Samuel Sharpe

The Rosetta Stone in hieroglyphics and greek

with translations and an explanation of the hieroglyphical characters, followed by

an Appendix of Kings' Names

Samuel Sharpe

The Rosetta Stone in hieroglyphics and greek
with translations and an explanation of the hieroglyphical characters, followed by an Appendix of Kings' Names

ISBN/EAN: 9783742844828

Manufactured in Europe, USA, Canada, Australia, Japa

Cover: Foto ©Andreas Hilbeck / pixelio.de

Manufactured and distributed by brebook publishing software (www.brebook.com)

Samuel Sharpe

The Rosetta Stone in hieroglyphics and greek

THE

ROSETTA STONE,

IN

HIEROGLYPHICS AND GREEK;

WITH

TRANSLATIONS,

AND AN EXPLANATION OF THE HIEROGLYPHICAL CHARACTERS;

AND FOLLOWED BY AN

APPENDIX OF KINGS' NAMES.

By SAMUEL SHARPE,

AUTHOR OF "THE HISTORY OF EGYPT."

LONDON:
JOHN RUSSELL SMITH, 36, SOHO SQUARE.
1871.

WORKS BY THE AUTHOR.

The DECREE of CANOPUS, in Hieroglyphics and Greek; with Translations, and an Explanation of the Hieroglyphical Characters.

EGYPTIAN HIEROGLYPHICS, being an Attempt to Explain their Nature, Origin, and Meaning; with a VOCABULARY.

EGYPTIAN INSCRIPTIONS from the British Museum and other sources; 216 Plates, in Folio.

The EGYPTIAN ANTIQUITIES in the BRITISH MUSEUM described.

The ALABASTER SARCOPHAGUS of Oimenepthah I., with Plates by JOSEPH BONOMI.

The TRIPLE MUMMY-CASE of Aroeri-ao, with Plates by JOSEPH BONOMI.

The HISTORY of EGYPT, from the Earliest Times till the Conquest by the Arabs, in A.D. 640. Fifth Edition.

The CHRONOLOGY and GEOGRAPHY of ANCIENT EGYPT. with Plates by JOSEPH BONOMI.

ALEXANDRIAN CHRONOLOGY.

The CHRONOLOGY of the BIBLE.

The HISTORY of the HEBREW NATION and its LITERATURE.

The HEBREW SCRIPTURES TRANSLATED, being a Revision of the Authorized English Old Testament. Second Edition.

The NEW TESTAMENT TRANSLATED from Griesbach's Text Twelfth Thousand.

CRITICAL NOTES on the Authorized English Version of the New Testament. Second Edition.

HISTORIC NOTES on the Books of the Old and New Testaments. Second Edition.

TEXTS from the HOLY BIBLE, explained by the Help of the Ancient Monuments. Second Edition.

EGYPTIAN MYTHOLOGY and EGYPTIAN CHRISTIANITY, with their Influence on the Opinions of Modern Christendom.

THE ROSETTA STONE.

INTRODUCTION.

In 1837 the Writer, following in the footsteps of Dr. Young and M. Champollion, published, in a work entitled " Egyptian Inscriptions from the British Museum and other sources," the Hieroglyphics of the Rosetta Stone, with an English translation. This fragment of fourteen broken lines, accompanied with its Greek translation, remained the small portion of hieroglyphical writing upon which our power of reading other Inscriptions rested, until the late discovery of the Decree of Canopus, which is also accompanied with a Greek translation. This latter Inscription contains thirty-seven unbroken lines; and in it the number of translated words is not only larger in the proportion of its length, but they are also understood with greater certainty, since they are not interrupted by gaps. Moreover, though the Decree of Canopus is not on hard basalt, like the Rosetta Stone, but on far softer limestone, yet its characters are less broken, and are in few cases open to any doubt. Hence, with the knowledge gained from that new source, the student naturally turns to a new examination of the Rosetta Stone, and thus finds that he is able to overcome difficulties and to remove doubts which had before troubled him. And yet further, the unbroken characters of the Decree of Canopus enable us to copy more correctly the Rosetta Stone. Some of its characters, which have been injured by time, can now be copied with greater certainty.

These are the Writer's reasons for again publishing the Hieroglyphics of the Rosetta Stone, which he does in a form corresponding to his publication of the Decree of Canopus. He has taken upon himself to divide the hieroglyphical lines into words, and has numbered each word for the convenience of referring to it in the Explanation which follows. That the reader may understand how much of the Inscription is wanting, the broken space at the end of each line is left of its proper length. In one case only is that space filled up conjecturally—namely, between lines seven and eight.

As he did in publishing the Decree of Canopus, so here the Writer adds the Greek copy of the Decree, then translations of the Greek and of the Hieroglyphics in opposite pages, showing how far they correspond one to the other, and, lastly, an Explanation of the Hieroglyphical Characters, in which he endeavours to support the rendering which he gives to each word by comparing it with the Coptic language, and also by referring to the various places in these two Decrees in which it must bear the same meaning. He has made no attempt to reduce his translation of the Hieroglyphics into good English, leaving the disjointed sentences to show in some cases the uncertainty of the rendering, and in other cases the very loose way in which the scribe has expressed himself.

The Decree is dated at Memphis on the 25th March, B.C. 196, making use of the wandering year which then began on the 11th October, and taking no notice of the reformation of the Calendar which had been proposed in the Decree of Canopus forty-two years earlier.

An Appendix contains a number of Kings' names. These, as they can be compared with the well-known names in the Greek historians, give us the alphabetic force of a large number of Hieroglyphics. They are arranged in chronological order; but for our purpose they should be studied backwards, because the modern names give us the more certain key by which the older names are read. As the Author has published the Alphabet with the Decree of Canopus, and also in his "Egyptian Hieroglyphics," he does not repeat it here. The reader can easily make it for himself.

Thus, with these Kings' names, and the two translated Decrees, and with the Coptic Lexicon, the student has a safe base from which he may start in his hieroglyphical inquiries.

During the half-century which has passed between the publication of the first and of the second of these translated Inscriptions, a knowledge of many other words has been gained from other sources. The meaning of some has been learned from the pictures which they accompany, and has been confirmed by the Coptic Lexicon. Others are explained by the Determinative Sign, or the pictorial nature of the group of letters. But unfortunately this knowledge has been overlaid by a number of ingenious but unproved guesses, many of which may now be brought to the test of the greater certainty which can be gained from the Decree of Canopus. This re-examination of received opinions, this going to school again, is, however, a troublesome task, which some minds do not readily submit to. Hence the cold reception of the Decree of Canopus, and the unfavourable opinion expressed of the Author's publication in some Reviews. One critic says, " We have got beyond all that." Another calls the Author's publication " a mischievous work," as unsettling the received and " orthodox " opinions. A third thinks that what we learn from the Decree of Canopus, and its Greek translation, should be judged by the results which ingenuity may have derived from the untranslated Inscriptions, and would thus try to decypher the *ignotum per ignotius*. All this time, however, while doubts hang over the reading of many Egyptian sentences, greater certainty is being established in other results; and from the improved condition of Egypt we may yet hopefully look forward to the future discovery of other translated Inscriptions, not to remove all difficulties in reading Hieroglyphics, but to increase the quantity of what is certainly known.

IN THE FOLLOWING PAGES

D.S. means the Determinative Sign, the pictorial figure, often following a word spelt by letters, and explaining it.

Voc. means the Vocabulary accompanying the author's "Egyptian Hieroglyphics."

CORRECTIONS FOR THE AUTHOR'S DECREE OF CANOPUS.

Page 32.

22 Perhaps THOSE WHO ROBE ; S,ME,R,?,U, from ⲗⲗⲏⲡ, *to bind on.* See No. 30, 13, for the same word.

1 The GODS, according to the Greek, and according to No. 30, 14; but more literally the HAPPY ONES, from ⲟⲩⲣⲱⲧ, *joy.* See *His Majesty,* No. 3, 18.

2 WITH ROBES or COLLARS ; the preposition M, followed by an ornamental collar. For these corrections I am indebted to the *North British Review.*

Page 41.

40 *Add;* the K,N, may be ⲕⲏⲛ, *income.*

Page 56.

12 BECAUSE OF ALL ; S,N,I,B ; Ϭⲉ, *therefore,* and ⲛⲓⲃⲓ, *all.* See ⲛⲓⲃⲓ, No. 30, 34. At No. 13, 28, WHEREAS is required for this group. The use of the word "All" in this group may be explained by our word " Al-though."

13 Perhaps WHICH ; R,T,A, ⲁⲅⲡⲟⲧⲉ. This meaning seems required several times in the Rosetta Stone. See also No. 29, 43.

14 Perhaps SIGNS ; M,N,E, with S,N, for the plural. But the Greek requires " It seemed fit."

15 UNTO; A,N ; ⲛ̄, as No. 32, 30, and 35, 26.

Page 62.

28 WHEREAS, literally WHICH, as No. 11, 12.

Page 102.

43 WHICH, as No. 11, 12.

1 To what Coptic word this corresponds is very doubtful.

Page 103.

13 THOSE WHO CLOTHE ; as No. 2, 22.

15 WITH ROBES or collars ; as No. 3, 2.

Page 119.

12 This enchorial portion was executed on the edge of the stone. On the face are only cut two out of the three portions.

Plate 1.

line 1.

THE

HIEROGLYPHICAL INSCRIPTION

ON

THE ROSETTA STONE.

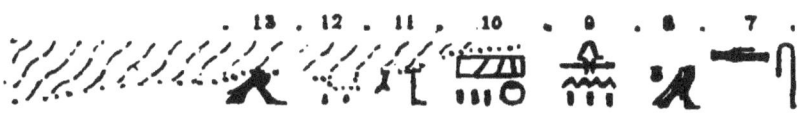

2.

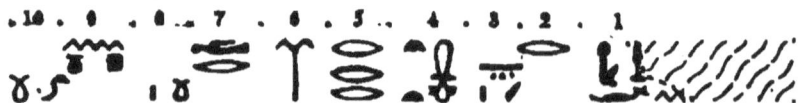

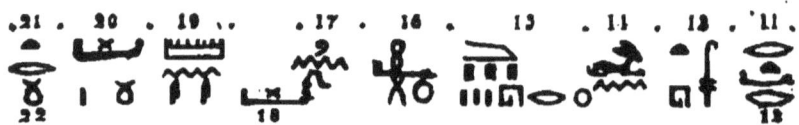

3.

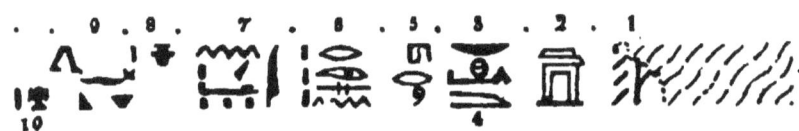

Plate 3. ROSETTA STONE. lines 4, 5.

4.

5.

6

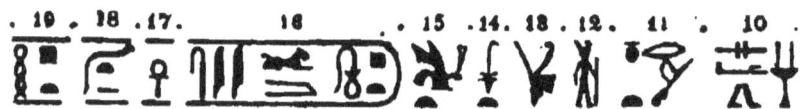

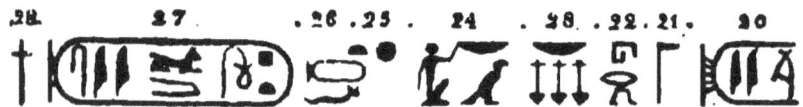

7

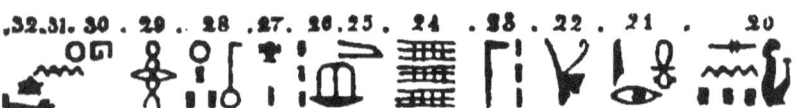

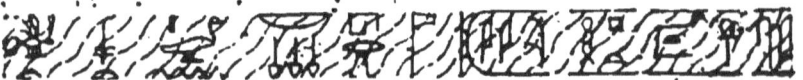

Plate 5.   ROSETTA STONE.   lines 8, 9.

8.

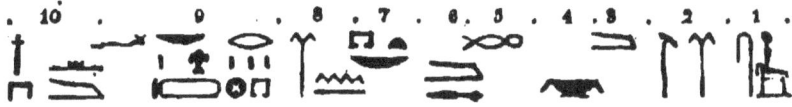

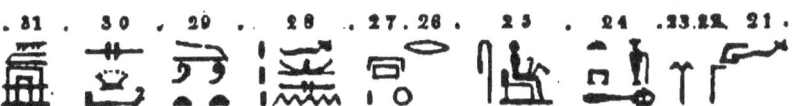

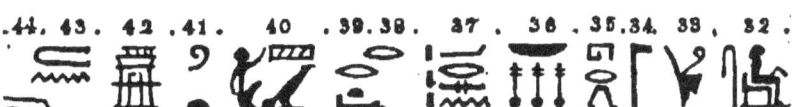

9.

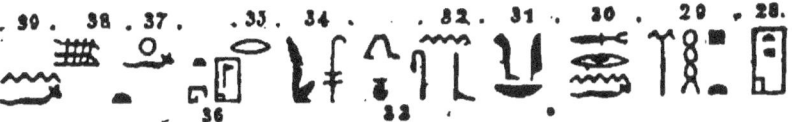

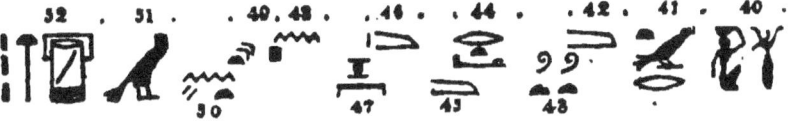

Plate 7.   ROSETTA STONE.   lines 12, 13.

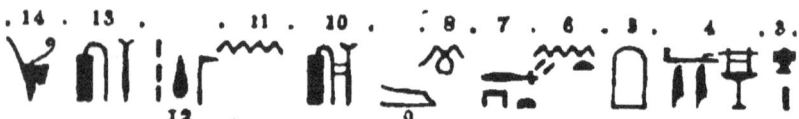

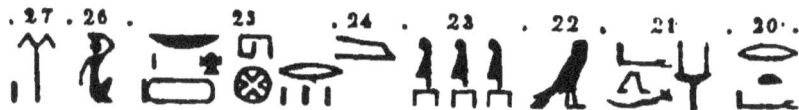

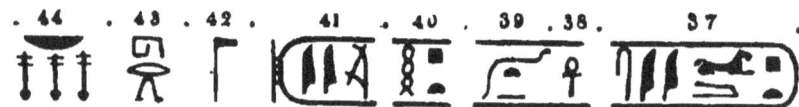

THE ROSETTA STONE

IN THE BRITISH MUSEUM.

---

1 Βασιλευοντος του νεου και παραλαβοντος την βασιλειαν
παρα του πατρος, κυριου βασιλειων, μεγαλοδοξου, του την
Αιγυπτον καταστησαμενου· και τα προς τους

2 θεους ευσεβους, αντιπαλων υπερτερου, του τον βιον των
ανθρωπων επανορθωσαντος, κυριου τριακονταετηριδων, καθαπερ ὁ Ἡφαιστος ὁ μεγας, βασιλεως, καθαπερ ὁ Ἡλιος

3 μεγας βασιλευς, των τε ανω και των κατω χωρων, εκγονου
θεων Φιλοπατορων, ὁν ὁ Ἡφαιστος εδοκιμασεν, ᾧ ὁ Ἡλιος
εδωκεν την νικην, εικονος ζωσης του Διος, υιου του Ἡλιου,
Πτολεμαιου,

4 αιωνοβιου, ηγαπημενου υπο του Φθα, ετους ενατου, εφ᾽ ιερεως
Αετου του Αετου Αλεξανδρου και θεων Σωτηρων και θεων
Αδελφων και θεων Ευεργετων και θεων Φιλοπατορων και

5 θεου Επιφανους Ευχαριστου, αθλοφορου Βερενικης Ευεργε-
τιδος Πυρρας της Φιλινου, κανηφορου Αρσινοης Φιλαδελφου
Αρειας της Διογενους, ιερειας Αρσινοης Φιλοπατορος Ειρηνης

6 της Πτολεμαιου, μηνος Ξανδικου τετραδι, Αιγυπτιων δε
Μεχειρ οκτωκαιδεκατῃ· Ψηφισμα·
Οἱ αρχιερεις και προφηται και οἱ εις το αδυτον ει[ς] πορευο-
μενοι προς τον στολισμον των

7 θεων και πτεροφορ[ο]ι και ιερογραμματεις και οἱ αλλοι ιερεις
παντες οἱ απαντησαντες εκ των κατα την χωραν ιερων εις
Μεμφιν τῳ βασιλει προς την πανηγυριν της παραληψεως
της

B

8 βασιλειας της Πτολεμαιου, αιωνοβιου, ηγαπημενου υπο του
Φθα, θεου Επιφανους Ευχαριστου, ην παρελαβεν παρα του
πατρος αυτου, συναχθεντες εν τῳ εν Μεμφει ιερῳ τη ημερᾳ
ταυτῃ ειπαν·

9 Επειδη βασιλευς Πτολεμαιος, αιωνοβιος, ηγαπημενος υπο
του Φθα, θεος Επιφανης Ευχαριστος, ο εγ Βασιλεως Πτολεμαιου και βασιλισσης Αρσινοης, θεων Φιλοπατορων, κατα
πολλα ευεργετηκεν τα θ ιερα και

10 τους εν αυτοις οντας και τους υπο την εαυτου βασιλειαν
τασσομενους απαντας, υπαρχων θεος εκ θεου και θεας, καθαπερ
Ωρος ο της Ισιος και Οσιριος υιος, ο επαμυνας τῳ πατρι
αυτου Οσιρει, τα[τε] προς θεους

11 ενεργετικως διακειμενος ανατεθεικεν εις τα ιερα αργυρικας
τε και σιτι[κ]ας προσοδους και δαπανας πολλας υπομεμενηκεν
ενεκα του την Αιγυπτον εις ευδιαν αγαγειν και τα ιερα
καταστησασθαι,

12 ταις τε εαυτου δυναμεσιν πεφιλανθρωπηκε πασαις, και απο
των υπαρχουσων εν Αιγυπτῳ προσοδων και φορολογιων τινας
μεν εις τελος αφηκεν, αλλας δε κεκουφικεν. οπως ο τε λαος
και οι αλλοι παντες εν

13 ευθηνιᾳ ωσιν επι της εαυτου βασιλειας, τα τε βασιλικα
οφειληματα α προσωφειλον οι εν Αιγυπτῳ και οι εν τη λοιπη
βασιλειᾳ αυτου, οντα πολλα τῳ πληθει αφηκεν, και τους εν
ταις φυλακαις

14 απηγμενους και τους εν αιτιαις οντας εκ πολλου χρονου
απελυσε των ενκεκλημενων, προσεταξε δε και τας προσοδους
των ιερων και τας διδομενας εις αυτα κατ᾽ ενιαυτον συνταξεις
σιτι-

15 κας τε και αργυρικας, ομοιως δε και τας καθηκουσας απομοιρας
τοις θεοις απο τε της αμπελιτιδος γης και των παραδεισων
και των αλλων των υπαρξαντων τοις θεοις επι του πατρος
αυτου

16 μενειν επι χωρας· προσεταξεν δε και περι των ιερεων όπως
μηθεν πλειον διδωσιν εις το τελεστικον ού ετασσοντο έως
του πρωτου ετους επι του πατρος αυτου· απελυσεν δε και
τους εκ των

17 ιερων εθνων του κατ' ενιαυτον εις Αλεξανδρειαν καταπλου·
προσεταξεν δε και την συλληψιν των εις την ναυτειαν μη
ποιεισθαι, των τ' εις το βασιλικον συντελουμενων εν τοις
ιεροις βυσσινων

18 οθονιων απελυσεν τα δυο μερη, τα τε εγλελειμμενα παντα εν
τοις προτερον χρονοις αποκατεστησεν εις την καθηκουσαν
ταξιν φροντιζων όπως τα ειθισμενα συντεληται τοι[ς] θεοις
κατα το

19 προσηκον, όμοιως δε και το δικαιον πασιν απενειμεν, καθαπερ
Ἑρμης ὁ μεγας και μεγας·
πρ[ο]σεταξεν δε και τους καταπορευομενους εκ τε των μαχι-
μων και των αλλων των αλλοτρια

20 φρονησαντων εν τοις κατα την ταραχην καιροις κατελθοντας
μενειν επι των ιδιων κτησεων· προενοηθη δε και όπως εξαπος-
ταλωσιν δυναμεις ιππικαι τε και πεζικαι και νηες επι τους
επελθοντας

21 επι την Αιγυπτον κατα τε την θαλασσαν και την ηπειρον
υπομεινας δαπανας αργυρικας τε και σιτικας μεγαλας, όπως
τα θ'ιερα και οί εν αυτη παντ[ε]ς εν ασφαλεια ωσιν·
παραγινομε-

22 νος δε και εις Λυκων πολιν την εν τῷ Βουσιριτῃ, ή ην κατει-
λημμενη και ωχυρωμενη προς πολιορκιαν όπλων τε παρα-
θεσει δαψιλεστερα και τη αλλη χορηγια παση, ώς αν εκ
πολλου

23 χ[ρ]ονου συνεστηκυιας της αλλοτριοτητος τοις επισυναχ-
θεισιν εις αυτην ασεβεσιν, οί ησαν εις τε τα ιερα και τους
εν Αιγυπτῳ κατοικουντας πολλα κακα συντετελεσμενοι,
και αν-

24 τικαθισας χωμασιν τε και ταφροις και τειχεσιν αυτην
αξιολογοις περιελαβεν· του τε Νειλου την αναβασιν μεγαλην
ποιησαμενου εν τῳ ογδοῳ ετει και ειθισμενου κατακλυ-
ζειν τα

25 πεδια, κατεσχεν εκ πολλων τοπων οχυρωσας τα στοματα
των ποταμων, χορηγησας εις αυτα χρηματων πληθος ουκ
ολιγον και καταστησας ἱππεις τε και πεζους προς τῃ
φυλακῃ

26 αυτων εν ολιγῳ χρονῳ την τε πολιν κατα κρατος εἱλεν και
τους εν αυτῃ ἀσεβεις παντας διεφθειρεν, καθαπερ ['Ερμ]ης
και Ωρος ὁ της Ισιος και Οσιριος υἱος εχειρωσαντο τους εν
τοις αυτοις

27 τοποις αποστανταςπροτερον, τους [δ'] αφηγησαμενους των
αποσταντων επι του ἑαυτου πατρος και την χωραν ε[νοχλησ]-
αντας και τα ἱερα αδικησαντας παραγενομενος εις Μεμφιν
επαμυνων

28 τῳ πατρι και τῃ ἑαυτου βασιλειᾳ παντας εκολασεν καθηκον-
τως καθ᾽ ὃν καιρον παρεγενηθη προς το συντελεσθη[ναι αυτῳ
τα] προσηκοντα νομιμα τῃ παραληψει της βασιλειας· αφηκεν
δε και τα ε[ν]

29 τοις ἱεροις οφειλομενα εις το βασιλικον ἑως του ογδοου ετους,
οντα εις σιτου τε και αργυριου πληθος ουκ ολιγον· ὡσαυ[τως
δε κ]αι τας τιμας των μη συντετελεσμενων εις το βασιλικον
βυσσινων οθ[ονι]-

30 ων και των συντετελεσμενων τα προς τον δειγματισμον
διαφορα ἑως των αυτων χρονων· απελυσεν δε τα ἱερα και
της [αποτεταγ]μενης αρταβης τῃ αρουρᾳ της ἱερας γης, και
της αμπελιτιδος ὁμοι[ως]

31 το κεραμιον τῃ αρουρᾳ· τῳ τε Απει και τῳ Μνευει πολλα
εδωρησατο και τοις αλλοις ἱεροις ζῳοις τοις εν Αιγυπτῳ,
πολυ κ[ρε]ισσον των προ αυτου βασιλεων φροντιζων ὑπερ
των ανηκον[των εις]

32 αυτα δια παντος, τα τ' εις τας ταφας αυτων καθηκοντα διδους
δαψιλως και ενδοξως, και τα τελισκομενα εις τα ιδια ιερα
μετα θυσιων και πανηγυρεων και των αλλων των νομι-
[ζομενων],

33 τα τε τιμια των ἱερων και της Αιγυπτου διατετηρηκεν επι
χωρας ακολουθως τοις νομοις, και το Απιειον εργοις πολυ-
τελεσιν κατεσκυασεν χορηγησας εις αυτο χρυσιου τε κ[αι
αργυρι·]

31 ου και λιθων πολυτελων πληθος ουκ ολιγον· και ἱερα και
ναους και βωμους ἱδρυσατο, τα τε προσδεομενα επισκευης
προσδιωρθωσατο εχων θεου Ενεργετικου εν τοις ανηκο[υσιν
εις το]

35 θειον διανοιαν· προσπυνθανομενος τε τα των ἱ[ε]ρων τιμιω-
τατα αν[ε]νεουτο επι της ἑαυτου βασιλειας, ὡς καθηκει, ανθ'
ὡν δεδωκασιν αυτῳ οἱ θεοι ὑγιειαν, νικην, κρατος και τ'αλλ'
αγαθ[α παντα],

36 της βασιλειας διαμενουσης αυτῳ και τοις τεκνοις εις τον
ἁπαντα χρονον· αγαθη τυχῃ·
εδοξεν τοις ἱερευσι των κατα την χωραν ἱερων παντων τα
ὑπαρχοντα τ[ιμια συντελεσαι]

37 τῳ αιωνοβιῳ βασιλει Πτολεμαιῳ, ηγαπημενῳ ὑπο του Φθα,
θεῳ Ε[π]ιφανει Ευχαριστῳ, ὁμοιως δε και τα των γονεων
αυτου, θεων Φιλ[ο]πατορων, και τα των προγονων, θεων
Ενεργ[ετων, και τα]

38 των θεων Αδελφων και τα των θεων Σωτηρων επαυξειν
μεγαλως· στησαι δε του αιωνοβιου βασιλεως Πτο[λε]μαιου
θεου Επιφανους Ευχαριστου εικονα εν ἑκαστῳ ἱερῳ εν τῳ
επιφα[νεστατῳ τοπῳ],

39 ἡ προσονομασθησεται Πτολεμαιου τον επαμυναντος τῃ
Αιγυπτῳ, ῇ παρεστηξεται ὁ κυριωτατος θεος του ἱερου διδους
αυτῳ ὁπλον νικητικον, ἁ εσται κατεσκευασμεν[α τον των
Αιγυπτιων]

40 τροπον, και τους ιερεις θεραπευειν τας εικονας τρις της
ημερας και παρατιθεναι αυταις ιερον κοσμον και τ'αλλα τα
νομιζομενα συντελειν, καθα και τοις αλλοις θεοις εν [ταις
κατα την χωραν πα]-

41 νηγυρεσιν· ιδρυσασθαι δε βασιλει Πτολεμαιῳ, θεῳ Επιφανει
Ευχαριστῳ, τῳ εγ βασιλεως Πτολεμαιου και βασιλισσης
Αρσινοης, θεων Φιλοπατορων, ξοανον τε και ναον χρ[υσουν
εν εκαστῳ των]

42 ιε[ρ]ων και καθιδρυσαι εν τοις αδυτοις μετα των αλλων ναων
και εν ταις μεγαλαις πανηγυρεσιν, εν αις εξοδειαι των
ναων γινονται, και τον θεου Επιφανους Ευ[χαριστου ναον
συνε]-

43 ξοδενειν· οπως δ' ευσημος ῃ νυν τε και εις τον επειτα χρονον,
επικεισθαι τῳ ναῳ τας του βασιλεως χρυσας βασιλειας δεκα,
αις προσκεισεται ασπις, [καθαπερ και επι πασων]

44 των ασπιδοειδων βασιλειων των επι των αλλων ναων· εσται
δ' αυτων εν τῳ μεσῳ ἡ καλουμενη βασιλεια Ψχεντ, ἡν περι-
θεμενος εισηλθεν εις το εν Μεμφ[ει ιερον οπως εν αυτῳ
συν]-

45 τελεσθη τα νομιζομενα τῃ παραληψει της βασιλειας· επι-
θειναι δε και επι του περι τας βασιλειας τετραγωνου κατα το
προειρημενον βασιλειον φυλακτηρια χρ[υσα δεκα, οις εγγραφ-
θησεται ὁ]

46 τι εστιν του βασιλεως του επιφανη ποιησαντος την τε ανω
χωραν και την κατω·
και επι την τρια[κ]αδα του Μεσορη, εν ῃ τα γενεθλια του
βασιλεως αγεται, ὁμοιως δε και [την ἑπτακαιδεκατην του
Μεχειρ],

47 εν ῃ παραλαβεν την βασιλειαν παρ[α] του πατρος, επωνυμους
νενομικασιν εν τοις ιεροις, αἱ δη πολλων αγαθων αρχηγοι
[π]ασιν εισιν, αγειν τας ἡμερας ταυτας εορτ[ην και πανηγυριν
εν τοις κατα την Αι]-

48 γυπτον ιεροις κατα μηνα, και συντελειν εν αυτοις θυσιας και
σπονδας και τ'αλλα τα νομιζομενα καθα και εν ταις αλλαις
πανηγυρεσιν, τας τε γινομενας προθε[σεις . . . . . .
. . . . πα]-

49 ρεχομενοις εν τοις ιεροις· αγειν δε εορτην και πανηγυριν τω
αιωνοβιω και ηγαπημενω υπο του Φθα βασιλει Πτολεμαιω
θεω Επιφανει και Ευχαριστω κατ' ενι[αυτον εν τοις ιεροις·
τοις κατα την]

50 χωραν απο της νουμηνιας του Θωυθ εφ' ημερας πεντε, εν δις
και στεφανηφορησουσιν συντελουντες θυσιας και σπονδας και
τ'αλλα τα καθηκοντα, προσαγορε[υεσθαι δε τους ιερεις των
αλλων θεων]

51 και του θεου Επιφανους Ευχαριστου ιερεις [π]ρος τοις αλλοις
ονομασιν των θεων ων ιερατευουσι, και καταχωρισαι εις
παντας τους χρηματισμους και εις τους α[λλους . . . .
. . . . την]

52 ιερατειαν αυτου· εξειναι δε και τοις αλλοις ιδιωταις αγειν
την εορτην και τον προειρημενον ναον ιδρυεσθαι και εχειν
παρ' αυτοις συντελο[υντας τα νομιμα εν εορταις ταις τε κατα
μηνα και τ-

53 αι]ς κατ' ενιαυτον, οπως γνωριμον η, διοτι οι εν Αιγυπτω
αυξουσι και τιμωσι τον θεον Επιφανη Ευχαριστον βασιλεα
καθαπερ νομιμον εστ[ιν αυτοις·
το δε ψηφισμα τουτο αναγραψαι εις στη-

54 λας σ]τερεου λιθου τοις τε ιεροις και εγχωριοις και Ελλη-
νικοις γραμμασιν και στησαι εν εκαστω των τε πρωτων και
δευτερων [και τριτων ιερων προς τη του αιωνοβιου βασιλεως
εικονι.

ROSETTA STONE,

FROM THE GREEK.

.

1   In the reign of the young man, on his taking up the kingdom
from his father, the glorious lord of kingdoms, the estab-
2   lisher of Egypt, pious in matters of religion, superior to his
enemies, regulator of the life of men, lord of the cycles of
3   thirty years, like Hephæstus the great king, like the Sun, the
great king of the upper and lower regions, son of the gods
Philopatores, whom Hephæstus approved, to whom the Sun
gave victory, a living image of Jupiter, son of the Sun,
4   Ptolemy, immortal, beloved by Phtha,—in the ninth year;

    Aetes, the son of Aetes, being priest of Alexander, and of
the gods Soteres, and of the gods Adelphi, and of the gods
Euergetæ, and of the gods Philopatores, and of the god
5   Epiphanes most gracious; Pyrrha, the daughter of Philinus,
being prize-bearer of Berenice Euergetis; Areia, the daughter
of Diogenes, being basket-bearer of Arsinoë Philadelphus;
6   Eirene, the daughter of Ptolemy, being priestess of Arsinoë
Philopator;

    On the fourth day of the [Macedonian] month Xandicus,
on the eighteenth day of the Egyptian month Mecheir,——
A Decree;

    The high priests and the prophets, and those who enter the
7 sanctuary on the robing of the gods, and the Pterophoræ, and the
sacred scribes, and all the other priests assembled at Memphis from
the temples of the land, to meet the king at the ceremony of
8 taking up the kingdom of Ptolemy immortal, beloved by Phtha,
god Epiphanes most gracious, which he received from his father,
being assembled in the temple at Memphis on the day aforesaid,
declared:

.

9 WHEREAS King Ptolemy immortal, beloved by Phtha, god
Epiphanes most gracious, son of King Ptolemy and Queen Arsinoë,
gods Philopatores, has in many things benefited the temples and
10 those who are in them, and all who are in office in his kingdom,
being a god, the son of a god and of a goddess, like Horus the
son of Isis and of Osiris, the avenger of his father Osiris, being
11 benevolently disposed towards divine affairs, has laid in the
temples tributes of silver and corn; and has incurred great ex-
penses for the sake of bringing Egypt into a state of tranquillity;
12 and of establishing the temples; and has benevolently exerted
himself with all his powers; and of the existing tributes in Egypt,
and dues, some he has altogether remitted, others he has lightened,
13 so that the people and all others should be happy throughout his
kingdom; he has remitted numerous debts to the crown which
those in Egypt and those in rest of the kingdom owed; those who
14 were confined in prison, and those who had been long under accu-
sations, he dismissed; and ordered that the tributes to the temples
15 and the taxes paid to them yearly in corn and silver, as well as the
accustomed portions to the gods from the vineyards, the gardens,
16 and the other places which belonged to the gods, under his father,
should continue throughout the region; and he ordered, with
respect to the priests, that they should give no more towards the
17 quota with which they were taxed for the first year [than] under
his father; he released those of the sacred classes from the annual
voyage to Alexandria; he ordered that the pressing for the navy
18 should not be carried on; of the linen cloths manufactured in the
temples for the king's use he remitted two parts; and all other
things he settled as in former times, in the accustomed order,
taking care that the accustomed services should be performed to
19 the gods, as was fit.

In the same way he dealt out justice to all, like the great-great
Hermes; and he ordered that those who returned from taking
20 arms, and of the others who plotted treason in the times of con-
fusion, those who returned, should remain upon their estates; and
he considered how the horse and foot forces and ships might be
21 sent against the invaders of Egypt, by sea and land, incurring a

great expense in silver and corn, that the temples and all the inha-
22 bitants of it [Egypt] might be in safety; and going against Lyco-
polis in the Busirite [Nome], which had been taken and fortified for
a siege, and largely provided with a supply of arms and all other
23 ammunition as if the impious persons congregated in it had been
for a long time of a settled disaffection, and had been con-
triving many evils against the temples and the inhabitants of
24 Egypt, having sat down before it, he surrounded it with mounds
and ditches and walls of remarkable extent; and on the great rise
25 of the Nile in the eighth year, flooding the plains as usual, he
held it back in many places, damming up the mouths of the rivers,
having provided not a small quantity of materials for that purpose,
26 and having set a guard upon them of horse and foot, in a short
time he took the city by force, and destroyed all the impious
persons in it; as [Hermes] and Horus the son of Isis and of
27 Osiris worsted in the same place the former rebels.

As to those who were the leaders of the rebels in the time of
his father, and who had laid waste the region and injured the
28 temples; coming down to Memphis, avenging his father, and his
kingdom, he punished them all as became the occasion, when he
came down to complete the appointed ceremonies on the taking up of
29 kingdom. He remitted what was owing from the temples to the
royal treasury up to the eighth year, which was not a small amount
30 of corn and silver, as also the royalties on the linen cloths, which
were not woven for the royal use, and the duties on those woven
as a specimen during the same period; he released the temples
from the debt of an artaba by the acre of the sacred land, and of
31 the Keramion by the acre of the vineyards; to Apis and Mnevis
he gave many things, and to the other sacred animals in Egypt,
much more than the kings before him did, caring for what
32 belonged to them in everything, and giving what was necessary
for their funerals largely and nobly, and the things requisite for
each of their temples for the sacrifices, and assemblies, and the
33 other appointed occasions. The honours of the temples and of
Egypt he preserved throughout the region according to the laws;
and he fitted up the temple of Apis with costly works, spending

ROSETTA STONE,

FROM THE HIEROGLYPHICS.

---

1 . . . . over the revenue; the regular soldiers, who rebelled, he struck down, so as not to remain . . . . . .

2 His majesty, of the land; [the duties on] the specimens, together with all the taxes, all the taxes on the fowls, which are belonging to the temples; the appointed Keramion by the acre of wine revenue; all the pasture revenue; the tax . . . . .

3 . . . . animals of the temples, regulating daily the cells as to their necessaries; he considered the temple-services for the funerals; therefore unto all other things for the cells, the great things for the . . . revenues unto him with good fortune . . . .

4 gold, and all other great libations according to the written laws of the temple of Tanis; which is for the living Apis, and an expense of gold, with silver, and precious stones, much expense he spent on

the living Apis in sufficiency.   He built temples, sanctuaries, altars, ...

5 . . . . religious ceremonies, behold, in a manner splendid; therefore unto him the immortal gods [gave] the revenues of victory, life, strength, and all other blessings of a great kingdom remaining unto himself and his children for ever—and with good fortune.

It was pleasing to the priests of the two regions, Upper and Lower Egypt . . . . .

6   together with the gods Soteres, who are gone to sleep, with religious ceremonies; in addition to set up a statue unto king Ptolemy living for ever, beloved by Pthah, god Epiphanes, lord of goodness, that it may be known by his other name as Ptolemy the defender of Egypt; each [time] he goes by water, Ptolemy . . . . .

7 . . . Egyptians shall serve the statue of the king [which stands beside] the statue which is in Tanis, three times in the day, upon it sacred ornaments, * * * * religious ceremonies for the offerings as unto the gods of the country in the assemblies on the holy days, upon the day of the festival, and also the day of his name; in addition to the ceremonies to make unto King Ptolemy . . . .

8   a portable statue, with an Anubis-staff, of gold, in each temple of Egypt * * * * * to be honoured together with the shrines of the gods of the country, to be done on the day of the great assemblies, at the going out of the god from the temple, the portable statue of Amun-Ra in his water processions, in addition shall carry out the shrine and portable statue of the god Epiphanes, lord of all blessings, by which it may be shown upon that same shrine . . . . .

. . . . .

9 . . . Every crown, the head of the shrine, the same in manner

them * * * shall be the crown called Pschent, which he wore
45 at Memphis when he entered the temple where the ceremonies
were performed on his taking up the kingdom. And there shall
be placed upon the square round about the crowns, near the
before-mentioned crown, golden phylacteries . . . . . .

46 . . . . that they are of the king who made the Upper and
the Lower regions illustrious.

And when the thirtieth day of Mesore, upon which the birthday of the king is kept, and the [seventeenth day of Paophi,] upon
47 which he took up the kingdom from his father, are sanctified with
his name in the temples, which days are the authors of many
blessings to us all, upon those days shall be celebrated a feast
48 * * * * in the temples of Egypt monthly,

and shall be performed in them sacrifices and libations, and the
other rites, as in the other festivals, and * * * * * *
49 held in the temples ;

and also there shall be a feast and a festival to the immortal and
beloved by Phtha, king Ptolemy, god Epiphanes most gracious,
50 yearly * * * * * * * through the region, from the
new moon of Thouth, during five days, on which the priests shall
wear crowns while offering sacrifices, libations, and other rites,
51 and the priests shall proclaim the name of Ptolemy . . . . . .
and god Epiphanes most gracious, in addition to the other names
of the gods whom they serve ; and they shall insert in all the formularies, and in the * * * * * *
52 * * of his priesthood ;

.   and it shall be lawful for other individuals to keep the
feast, and to make the above-mentioned shrine, and to have by
them * * * * * * * * *

as the two great asps, appointed on the head of the shrine a crown
upon it.   Because of which when   *   *   *   his illustrious
majesty went by boat from the palace at Memphis he entered
*   *   *   *   *   *   *   *   the chief priest of the temple, he took
the appointment unto himself of the great kingdom.   In addition
to which, in the place of the phylactery of silver which is on
. . . . . . which is on the square of the crown
10 . . . . of Lower Egypt, he celebrated the festival, he went by
boat, the sole monarch who made the Upper and Lower regions
illustrious.

Because of which it is decreed that the last day of Mesore, when
the birthday of the priest living for ever is kept in the assemblies
at the festival of Horus in the temples, it was done in like manner
upon the seventeenth day of Paophi, when he brought the treasures belonging to the chief priest, on the festival of the receiving
of the kingdom from his father; behold, it is the beginning of all
the other . . . .
11 . . . . place celebrated; which seventeen days, the last of every
month, in the assemblies in the temples of Egypt hereafter.   In
addition . . . . shall perform rites, and all other religious
honours, together with assemblies by boat, which shall be monthly,
and all other celebrations in the assemblies, which all scribes
*   *   *   of the god Horus in the temples. . . . .
12 . . . . Ptolemy living for ever, beloved by Phtha, god
Epiphanes, lord of goodness, yearly from the first day of Thoth,
during five days in every region, there shall be made an assembly
with altars, and shall celebrate rites, and all other religious ceremonies, on which the priests of the temples of the Egyptians shall
wear crowns during the proclamation of the Priest Epiphanes lord
of goodness; into the formularies. . . . .

13 *   *   *   the priesthood of god Epiphanes, lord of goodness,
on the signet rings on the hands of the priests; behold, it is made
very lawful to praise for appointed persons, who shall attend to
the altar, to set up a copy of that same shrine of god Epiphanes,
lord of goodness, by which it shall be lawful in the temples, in

D

53 yearly; so that it may be known why the Egyptians magnify and honour the god Epiphanes most gracious, as it is lawful.

54 *   *   *   *   * a tablet of hard stone in the sacred vulgar and Greek letters; and it shall be placed in each of the first, and the second * * *

     *   *   *   *   *   *   *

NOTE.—The conjectural additions to our Greek text are those of Boeckh, in his *Corpus Inscriptionum;* they are not always followed in our translation.

addition in all the festivals which are monthly and yearly; by which it is seen why it is lawful for the Egyptians that they should honour * * *

14 * * * * decrees, for which they shall set up a tablet which is in the temple, carved in letters for the priests, letters for books, and letters for Greek proclamations; which they shall set up in the temples of the Egyptians in a conspicuous place, on each first, each second, and each third of the base of the statue of King Ptolemy living for ever, beloved by Pthah, god Epiphanes, lord of goodness.

Line 1.

THESE few words should correspond with line 27 of the Greek.

1   The Dish, if without a handle, is NEB, perhaps meaning ⲛⲓⲃⲓ, *all*, an adjective following its substantive.

2   OVER; H,T,M; ϩⲁⲧⲙ̄, *over*. This Serpent is an H in ϩⲓⲛⲏϥ, line 6, 4; in ϩⲏⲧⲉⲛ, line 10, 21, and Canopus 27, 17; and in ϩⲓⲧⲟⲧ, Canopus 12, 17; in ϩⲱⲥ, Canopus 8, 38; and in several other less certain words. But it is not met with in the names of the Greek kings to give it the certainty desired. The Hand is a T in Trajan and Tiberius. This Cross is an M in Germanicus, but without the four dots which here accompany it.

3   REVENUE, or TAXES, as in line 2, 20. In Canopus 5, 40, the first two characters have this meaning when following K,N, perhaps ⲕⲏⲛ, *income*; and the arm holding the peculiar stick is figurative of *receiving*; in Canopus 3, 26, and 6, 5. The last two characters, SH,E, may be ⲥⲟ, *expense*, ⲥⲓ, *to take*, or ⲥⲉ, *to spend*. See line 2, 8, and 10. The Loop is an S in Domitianus, Germanicus, and Antoninus.

4   SOLDIERS, represented pictorially, with three dots, the usual sign of the plural.

5   APPOINTED, or REGULAR; SOT,N; ⲥⲟⲩⲧⲉⲛ, *to direct*, and followed by S, three dots, carelessly written for the usual S,N, three dots, the sign of the plural, as in the following word. This is the adjective to the foregoing substantive. The rabbit has this force seven times in this inscription, and fifteen times in that of Canopus. In Rosellini's Monumenti Civile, pl. 20, is a figure of the animal with its name written over it in hieroglyphics, SOAT. It takes this name from ⲥⲱⲧϩ *to burrow*; in Coptic ϧⲁⲣⲉⲥⲱⲟⲩⲧⲥ, literally *an under-burrower*.

6   Perhaps Who rebelled; M,T,E; with S,N, plural; ⲙⲁⲧⲟⲓ,
to fight. The three dots for the plural have the force of OU, a
form of the plural in Coptic. But the letters S,N, OU, are not
found in Coptic as a simple termination for nouns in the plural.
They are, however, too common in the hieroglyphics to be mis-
understood.

7   Perhaps He struck down; S,T; ϭⲟⲧ, *to strike.*

8, 9 A doubtful word; perhaps, M,M,N,T, with S,N, plural;
ⲉⲙⲟⲛⲧ, *not having;* or ⲉⲙ, *not,* and ⲙⲟⲛⲧ, *remaining;*
an adjective applied to the conquered rebels.

Line 2.

1   Probably His majesty. The F, ϥ, is the pronoun *his.* See
Canopus 3, 18, for a similar group.

2   Of; RO; a preposition common in the hieroglyphics; perhaps
ⲉⲁⲣⲟ. But see line 6, 2, where it is spelt H,RO.

3   The Land; T,O; ⲑⲟ, *the world.*

4   A pattern, or specimen; H,T,T; from ⲣⲉ, *like.* See line
13, 19. The tax on the specimens seems meant. See also line
10, 30, where it means *in like manner.*

5   R,R,R; ⲉⲣⲡⲁⲓ *with.* One R is in the place of the H; but
why there is a third R does not appear. See line 9, 20, for the
same word, and ⲉⲓⲣⲉⲛ in line 10, 31, for the same triple R in
place of HR. Compare the double R in Greek, ῤῥ, of which one
does little more than carry the aspirate.

6   M for ⲙⲛ. This and the last make a compound preposition,
together with.

7   All; T,R; ⲧⲏⲣ, as in lines 4, 5, and 8, 37. The first letter
is ⲧⲟⲧ, *a hand,* hence used for ⲧ.

8   Probably Taxes; SH,E; from ϭⲉ *to spend,* or ϭⲓ *to take.*
See line 1, 3, also below several times.

9   All; N,P,N; perhaps ⲛⲓⲃⲉⲛ. This custom of putting the
word *all* both before and after the substantive is very common.
See Canopus 30, 34 and 36. But here this word may belong
to the coming substantive.

10   Taxes on the fowls, if we may judge from the first character,
which is the head of a goose.

11   WHICH ; R,T,A ; perhaps ⲀⳒⲢⲞⲦⲈ, but not certainly traced in Coptic. See lines 5, 6, and 9, 44, and 13, 27.

12   OF, or BELONGING TO ; as in line 2, 2, &c.

13   TEMPLE, or PALACE ; S,T,E. The T may be either part of the word SOT, or the article to the word ⲎⲒ, *house*. See line 6, 14, for the word SOT as a priestly and royal title. The twig has the force of S, from ⲞⲈ, *a plant*.

14   APPOINTED, as in line 1, 5, &c.

15   KERAMION in the Greek ; CH,R,M,O,E,O, giving to the three dots their vowel sound. The first letter, the Ring, is usually R, from ⲢⲎ, *the sun*. To represent CH, it should have two strokes across it, which are here omitted, as also in the following word.

16   The ACRE ; CH,A,H ; ⲔⲀⲒⲈ, *a field*; compare also 10,2,1, *a field*.

17   Probably WINE ; O,N,T ; the Greek word οινον, as it would seem.

18   Probably REVENUE. See line 1, 3, also below, No. 20.

19   PASTURE ; M,N,I ; ⲙⲟⲛⲓ, *pasture*.

20   REVENUE or TAX, as in line 1, 3 ; a word compounded of No. 18 and No. 8.

21   ALL ; T,R ; ⲦⲎⲢ, as in lines 2, 7, and 4, 5, but with a T of another form.

22   Probably TAX ; the same as in line 2, 8, but without the final vowel.

23   Possibly part of the foregoing word.

Line 3.

1   ANIMALS ; TEB,O,E ; ⲦⲈⲂⲚⲎ, *an animal*. The finger ⲦⲈⲂ, is often the letter T, as in line 4, 5. But the first letter is doubtful.

2   TEMPLE, represented pictorially.

3   REGULATING ; as in Canopus 5, 31. The first character is ⲚⲎⲂ, *lord*, the others are the word *Steersman* in many inscriptions.

4   M ; it may be the prefix of the case for the following noun.

5   DAY or DAILY ; E,R,O, as in Canopus 13, 13 ; from ⲈⳒⲞⲞⲨ, *day*, and perhaps ⲢⲎ, *the sun*.

6   Possibly the CELLS, or chambers in the temple; R,I, with the
     termination S,N, plural; ⲡⲓ *a cell.* See line 3, 18, where the
     vowel is of a different form.

7   Possibly NECESSARIES ; A,N,K,E,A, plural; ⲛ̄ϭⲁⲓ, *necessary,*
     if the third letter is a ⲕ. In Cleopatra we have a triangle for ⲕ,
     but it is of a different form.

8, 9   Probably, HE CONSIDERED ; N,E,F,A,E,T, ⲛⲉⲁϥⲉⲓⲁⲧ.
     From ⲉⲓⲁⲧ, *to consider,* with ⲛⲉ ⲁϥ, the prefix of the tense
     and person.

10   THE; P,E; ⲡⲓ, the definite article as above. In Canopus this
     word is sometimes ⲏⲉ and sometimes THE.

11   Probably TEMPLE-SERVICES. See lines 11, 14, and 12, 30,
     where the ostrich feather, M, is an adjective over the word, *House,*
     and makes it into *Temple.*

12   FOR ; M ; ⲙ̄ⲛ̄, a preposition, as in line 4, 18.

13   FUNERALS ; T, CH, NEB ; from ⲧⲁⲕⲟ, *putridity.* The NEB
     may be ⲛⲓⲃⲓ, *all.*

14   THAT or WHICH, or THEREFORE ; as in lines 2, 11, and 5, 6 ;
     R,T,A ; ⲁⲍ̄ⲡⲟⲧⲉ.

15   UNTO ; N, the preposition, as in lines 5, 32, and 7, 31.

16   ALL OTHER ; ?,CH, T, NEB ; ⲕⲉⲧ, *other,* ⲛⲓⲃⲓ, *all.* The
     doubtful strokes with which this group begins may perhaps be
     those of line 4, 5.

17   THINGS FOR ; H,A,R,T, with S,N, plural; ⲍ̄ⲁⲣⲁⲧ, *for,* a pre-
     position here changed into a noun. See line 1, 2, for the force of
     the first letter.

18   The CELLS ; R,I ; ⲡⲓ, *a cell.* Compare No. 6, above.

19   THINGS FOR ; H,T, with S,N, plural ; ⲍ̄ⲏⲧ, *for,* another pre-
     position changed into a noun.

20   GREAT ; CH,R ; ϫⲟⲣ, *strong,* as in line 5, 19, where it is in
     the feminine. Though not in the plural, it may be the adjective
     to the foregoing substantive. The swallow has a similar force in
     ⲫⲁⲭⲉⲛ, Canopus 7, 28, and ⲥⲁⲫⲉⲙ, Canopus 7, 36.

21   WITH, AMONG ; O,T ; ⲟⲩⲧⲉ, as in line 5, 21.

22   A doubtful word, where the Greek gives no help ; I,R,O,T ;
     possibly ⲉⲣⲟⲩⲟⲧ, *joy,* also *income.*

23   Possibly INCOME; see lines 1, 3, and 2, 18.   Perhaps the first
character may belong to the foregoing word.

24   UNTO; N, the preposition, as in line 5, 32.

25   HIM; F; ᛘ.   See *His* in line 5, 26.

26   With GOOD FORTUNE; as in line 5, 29; but there it is followed
by the adjective *Good.*

27   A word of doubtful meaning.

28   The article; A,O; OⲨ, of frequent use in hieroglyphics, and
sometimes as the definite article, though in Coptic it is indefinite.

Line 4.

1   The Dish, without the additional character, would mean GOLD;
see line 8, 4.   It has the force of ΝΟⲨB, *gold*, in Noubkora,
the first name of Amunmai Thor II, which Eratosthenes reads
Chnubus Gneurus, and translates *Golden the son of Golden.*

2   AND; H,A; ΔѮΔ, as in line 5, 23, where the two letters are
joined.

3   LIBATIONS, represented pictorially by a jar pouring out water,
followed by three strokes for the plural termination.   Compare
Priests, line 12, 28.

4   GREAT; Ch, R, plural; ⲬOP, *strong*.   See also line 8, 20.
This is the adjective following its substantive.

5   ALL; T,R; THP; as in line 8, 37.   The first letter is THB
a finger, hence used for a T.   See line 9, 55.

6   OTHER, or literally OTHER ALL; CH,T, NEB; KEⲦ, *other*, and
ΝΙBEΙΙ *all*, as in line 5, 15.

7   ACCORDING TO, literally LIKE; H, ѮE, *like.*

8   The WRITINGS or LAWS; A,H, with S,N, plural.   The second
character is a roll of papyrus, ΔⳘΙ, *a rush*.   The Coptic word
is used in the Hebrew Bible, as אֲחוּ; see Genesis xli. 2 and 18,
and Job viii. 11.   See line 14, 15, where the roll of papyrus is
again used.

9   OF, the preposition R,O, as in line 5, 17, and 2, 2.

10   The TEMPLE.   The first character is a built house; the last is
the ground plan of a house, in this case, of the temple-yard.   It
is preceded by Ⲧ, the definite article feminine, to the word HΙ,
a house, which, however, in Coptic is masculine.

11   The name of a city; S,N, with the D.S. of a city. Probably
Tanis called Tsan ; but it might be Essè ; or even Sin, a name
given to Sais in Ezekiel xxx., 15.

12   Which ; N,T,E, Ⲛ̀ⲦⲈ, as in the name of Tiberius, No. 63 ;
and in Canopus, line 9, 44, &c.

13   Apis, the name of the sacred Bull of Memphis ; H,A,P ; as in
Canopus, 5, 26.

14   Living, the adjective following its substantive. It distinguishes
the Temple of the living bull, from the burial-place of those made
into mummies. See line 6, 17.

15   And ; H,A ; ⲁⲁ̣ⲁ. See line 4, 2.

16   Possibly Expense, or spending ; S,? ; perhaps ⲋⲟ, expense.
This seems required by the Greek.

17   Gold ; A,N,B ; ⲚⲞⲨⲂ ; followed by D.S. of a man putting a
crown on his head. See this B in the word ⲚⲞⲨⲎⲂ, priest, in
line 12, 35.

18   With ; M, for ⲙⲉⲛ.

19   Silver ; K,T ; ⲀⲀⲦ ; The D.S., as in the case of the word
Gold above, establishes the meaning of the word, though the
Greek is unfortunately injured in this place. The Coptic use of
the guttural explains how the K may stand for H.

20   Precious stones ; SH,T,N,O,S,O ; ⲰⲞⲦ, hard, and ⲈⲚⲈⲤⲈ,
beautiful. The sickle may have its force, S, from ⲰⲤⲀ, to reap.
See Canopus 11, 40. It is the first letter in 'Queen Scemiophra's
name, Appendix, No. 10.

21   Possibly Much ; SH,O,E,S ; the compound ⲰⲰ-ⲰⲰ,
each of which is much. See line 4, 31, for the force of the first
letter. It is when better formed the leaf of a water lily, and from
ⲋⲟ, a plant, has the force of SH. As a numeral it represents Ⲱⲁ,
a thousand.

22   M, the prefix, a noun's case, or of an infinitive mood.

23   Possibly Expense ; SH,E,M ; some form of ⲋⲟ, expense.
Compare lines 2, 10, and 2, 20.

24   Possibly He spent ; S,H,A,N,F. The F is ⳉ, he. In Coptic the
pronoun is prefixed, but in hieroglyphics it is postfixed. The

E

verb may be CA⳨NI, *to distribute.* But the second letter is doubtful.

25   APIS, as in line 4, 13.

26   LIVING, as in line 4, 14.

27   Possibly a SUFFICIENCY; R,S,A,S, may be a reduplicate form of pεϣ, *sufficient.*

28   Possibly HE BUILT; but one letter is of doubtful force, and one is injured. The word ends with ϥ, *he.*

29   TEMPLES, as in line 4, 10. Within the house is the hatchet, the character for *God,* as in line 6, 21.

30   SANCTUARIES, CH,M,?,T,E, plural; CH,M,?, may be ϧⲁⲙⲉ, *black,* meaning the dark rooms of the temple; T,E, plural, is from HI, *a house,* with the article prefixed, as in the preceding word.

31   ALTARS; SH,O; ϣϩοⲧⲓ, *an altar,* followed the D.S. See line 12, 21, also Canopus 20, 15, and 26, 12.

Line 5.

1   Perhaps part of the word Religious CEREMONY or OFFERING. See line 7, 20 and 39.

2   BEHOLD; A,S; IC; as in Canopus 19, 8.

3   IN; O,E, or E,O; ἐοⲧ, *in.* See line 7, 34.

4   MANNER; a character of uncertain force, but its meaning is well established by comparison with line 9, 8.

5   SPLENDID; SO,SO; ϣοⲧϣοⲧ. The twig, 6ⲟ̄, has this force in the word *King,* line 6, 14. Instead of these words, "In a manner splendid," the Greek has "as was fit."

6   THEREFORE, literally WHICH. The preposition *For* seems to have been omitted. See lines 13, 27, and 8, 39.

7   UNTO HIM; N,F; the preposition or prefix for the case n̄, followed by the pronoun ϥ.

8   The IMMORTAL GODS; the hatchet is the word ⲛοⲧⲧε, *god,* as in line 6, 21; the asp is often the determinative sign of a goddess, here used as an adjective. It has the force of a K in Caisaros, Appendix 69 and 70; and here may represent ⲭⲓⲏ, *power,* or ⲭⲱ, *lofty.*

9 Revenues; K,N,P,A; perhaps ⲔⲎⲚ, *revenues*. The arm is figurative of action. See Canopus 5, 40.

10   Of; N, the preposition, as in line 7, 41, &c.

11   Victory, according to the Greek; S,R,T; ⲞⲢⲎⲞⲨⲦ, followed by the two characters which also in No. 9 seemed superfluous. See line 9, 30, for the first letter.

12   Life, as in line 4, 14.

13   Strength, according to the Greek; but Good fortune in Canopus 10, 15, where the hook, S, precedes the other character instead of following it. The first character may be two letters; SH, with the crook, O, across it, and the word may then be ⲞⲞⳢⲒ, *eminence*.

14   All; T,R; ⲦⲎⲢ; as in line 4, 5.

15   Other, Ch,T—NEB; as in line 4, 6. The sculptor has not distinguished between the Ch, a ring with two strokes within it, and the R of No. 11, a ring with a dot in it.

16   Blessings. The first three characters may be translated Good, of, heaven; followed by S,N, three dots, for the plural. See *Good*, in line 6, 23; *Of*, in line 4, 9; and *Heaven*, in Canopus 20, 38, &c. This last is a picture of the arched vault.

17   Of; RO; as in line 4, 9, &c., and Canopus 4, 8, &c.

18   A kingdom; represented by a crowned man, preceded by a character which represents the Coptic ⲘⲉⲐ. This syllable changes a concrete into an abstract. See *Priesthood*, in line 13, 1. In Canopus 10, 41, &c., this character follows its noun.

19   Great, in the feminine singular. See Line 4, 4. The adjective following its substantive. The semicircle is T, the Coptic feminine article; in hieroglyphics, the inflexion of a feminine adjective. The substantives beginning with ⲘⲉⲐ are all feminine.

20   Remaining. The boundary stone is ⲦⲰⲨ, hence we have ⲦⲀϬⲦⲀϬ, *to remain*.

21   Unto; O,T; ⲞⲨⲦⲉ. See lines 3, 21, and 8, 41.

22   Himself; H,R,F; perhaps ⲈⲢⲀϥ, literally *his face*, the usual Coptic form for *himself*. The first letter here seems to be

the same as the first in line 4, 24; perhaps a beetle's head, an II, or TH.

23　AND; H,A; ⲁⳅⲁ; as in line 7, 33, &c.

24　CHILDREN; H,R,T; ϩⲣⲟⲧ, *a son.*

25　The determinative sign of the foregoing words being a child holding his fingers to his mouth, to show that he is too young to speak, with three dots for the plural. From this the Romans took their god of silence, Harpocrates, or Hor-pi-krot, *Horus the child.*

26　His, the pronoun adjective following its substantive F; ϥ. See line 5, 7.

27　FOR EVER; H,T,N; ϩⲏⲧⲉⲛ, *the end.* See line 6, 18, where the N is formed by a simple stroke, as in Canopus 1, 16.

28　AND; H,A; ⲁⳅⲁ, as in line 7, 33.

29　FORTUNE, or HAPPENING. By means of ϩⲛⲱⲧ, *the two arms,* the scribe represents the word ϩⲱⲧⲛ, *to happen.* See line 3, 26, and Canopus 30, 19.

30　GOOD, the adjective following its substantive; O,B; ⲟⲩⲁⲃ, *holy.* More often the latter character alone has this force, as at line 6, 23, &c. See Canopus 14, 1, where we have three letters to spell this word. For the B, see the name Scemiophra, Appendix, 10.

31　IT WAS PLEASING, according to the Greek, but the explanation of the group is uncertain.

32　UNTO; N, the preposition, as in line 5, 10, &c.

33　The PRIESTS, those who make libations to the gods, represented pictorially, and in the plural, as in line 12, 28.

34　OR; N,I; ⲛⲁ, *belonging to,* as in line 7, 4.

35　The TWO REGIONS; as in Canopus 3, 10, and 18, 7. Possibly from ⲕⲁⲧ, *a basket,* we may have ⲕⲁⳅⲓ, *a land.* The character may represent the serpent in a basket, as carried about in the Eleusinian processions, and represented on the coins of Asia Minor. See fig. The basket on the coin is that carried by the priestess mentioned in line 5 of the Greek of this Decree.

36   UPPER AND LOWER, the adjectives following their substantives.
The plants are distinctive of the two halves of Egypt, but the
difference is not shown upon an injured slab.

37   Probably SIMILAR ; H ; ⲅⲉ, *like*.

Line 6.

1   An imperfect word ending with R, and S,N, plural.

2   TOGETHER WITH ; H,R ; ⲅⲁⲣⲟ, as in line 7, 13, where these
two consonants are followed by a vowel.

3   The GODS SOTERES, Ptolemy Soter and his queen.   The
hatchet, from ⲛⲟⲩⲧ, *to bruise*, represents ⲛⲟⲩⲧⲉ, *a god*.   The
cross is CH, and is from ⲟⲩⲭⲁⲓ, *safety*.   See line 6, 28.   It is
the first letter in the word ⲭⲏⲗⲓ, line 13, 42.

4   ASLEEP, meaning DECEASED ; H,N,F ; ⲁⲓⲛⲏϭ, *sleep*.   See
line 5, 27, for the force of the first letter.

5   The figure of a mummy, with the plural sign, though the word
above is in the dual form.   It is the D.S. of the deceased
sovereigns.

6   WITH ; N, the preposition, as in line 5, 32, where the letter was of
a different form.   This crown is the Bright Plate of Exodus, xxxix.
30, and has it force from ⲟⲩⲉⲓⲛ, *light*.

7   RELIGIOUS CEREMONIES, as in Canopus 4, 7 ; T,O,T, with a
mummy, and S,N, plural ; from ⲧⲟⲩⲱⲧ, *an image* ; and therefore the ceremonies were honours paid to the dead.

8   IN ; M, the preposition, as in line 3, 12.

9   ADDITION ; O,T,O,T ; from ⲟⲩⲁⲅⲧⲟⲧ, *to add*.   See line 8,
29.   In Canopus this word is spelt ⲅⲓⲧⲟⲧ, as in the name of
Ptolemy Alexander ; Appendix 58.

10   To SET UP ; ?,S,A,T ; from ⲥⲉⲧ, *to place*, preceded by the
figure of an erection.

11   A STATUE.   The character is two arms holding a chisel, the
sculptor's tool, followed by N,T, which may be part of the word,
or may be ⲛⲉⲧ, *which*.   See line 14, 33.

12   The figure of the above statue wearing the crown.

13   UNTO ; N, the preposition, as in line 6, 6.

14   SOT, a priestly title of the highest rank, sometimes spelt *Soten*.
It is the *Sethon* of Herodotus II., 141, and *Sethos* of Manetho,

and by the latter used as a name for Rameses II., the *King*. It belonged more particularly to Upper Egypt.

15   Nout, a priestly title of the second rank, and of Lower Egypt. These two titles are usually united on the sovereign, and may be translated KING.

16   Ptolemy; P,T,O,L,M,A,A,S; *Ptolemæus.*

17   Living; O, for ⲟⲛⲟⲯ, *life*. See *Life*, line 5, 12.

18   For ever; H,T,N; ⲅ̇ⲏⲧⲉⲛ, *the end*, as in line 5, 27, where the N is properly formed.

19   Pthah, the great god of Memphis; P,T,H.

20   Beloved; M,A,A; ⲙⲉⲓ, *to love*. As the adjective follows the noun, the two words mean "By Pthah beloved." Had the order been changed, they would have meant "Loving Pthah." Thus far the king's titles which follow his name are included with it in the same oval ring.

21   God; ⲛⲟⲩⲧⲉ; as in line 6, 3. This word, when written in full, has the Hatchet followed by a T. The Hatchet alone, from ⲛⲉⲅ̇, *to strike*, represents only the first syllable.

22   Epiphanes, the well-known name of the fifth Ptolemy; E,R,T; the E for ⲉⲅ̇ⲟⲟⲩ, *day;* and the R,T, may be ⲉⲣⲏⲧ, *to promise.*

23   Gracious, or literally LORD OF GOODNESS; the dish, ⲛⲏⲃ, *lord*, and the B repeated three times for ⲟⲩⲁⲃ, *holy*, in the plural. See line 8, 36. Also see line 5, 30, where ⲟⲩⲁⲃ has the vowel at the beginning.

24   That it may be known, represented pictorially by a man holding forward a dish. Compare lines 8, 40, and 12, 34, and 14, 19.

25   Other; K,T; ⲕⲉⲧ, *other*, the adjective to the coming substantive.

26   Name his. The oval, within which a king's name is written, represents the word ⲣⲁⲛ, *a name;* the F, ϥ, is *His*.

27   Ptolemy; as above, line 6, 16.

28   The defender or saviour; as at line 6, 3.

29   Of; N,E; ⲛⲁ, *belonging to.*

30   Egypt. From ⲭⲁⲙⲉ, *black;* the eye, when so ornamented

with black paint, according to the custom of the Egyptian women, may represent ✗H𝚺𝚺I, *Egypt.* It is followed by 𝐓, the article, and the D.S. of a city or country. See Canopus 6, 12.

31 HIS BARGE, as would seem from the first character, or perhaps HIS GOING BY WATER. But the Greek does not help us.

32 Perhaps EACH ; P,O ; ΠΟΥ𝚫, *each;* as in Canopus 12, 9. The adjective to the foregoing substantive. But this word is uncertain. See line 10, 6.

33 PTOLEMY, as above.

34

Line 7.

1 EGYPTIANS. This group is not easily explained. E,K,NEB, P,I, RAN,F. The first syllable, RO, is here wanting. See lines 8, 9, and 14, 25, where its meaning is quite established.

2 SHALL HONOUR, or SERVE, according to the Greek. In Canopus 20, 22, and 33, 1, the S, the sign of the future tense, is prefixed. Here it is postfixed.

3 The STATUE, as in line 6, 11.

4 OF ; N,E ; 𝚗𝚫, *belonging to,* as in line 6, 29.

5 The KING ; as known by his crown. See line 6, 12.

6 A statue, as would seem from the Greek, by the side of which the king's statue is to be placed. Thus we have the two statues placed side by side, instead of a description of their position by means of writing, and we must read STANDING BESIDE THE *statue.* The thought is represented pictorially, as in the Mexican picture-writing.

7 WHICH, is the meaning required by the context, but neither the Greek text nor the Coptic language here help us. See lines 9, 53, and 11, 6, and 11, 35, where this meaning is also required for this group of letters, A,P,N. In Canopus 2, 15, this word is spelt without the vowel.

8 IN ; M, the preposition, or prefix of the case.

9 The CITY of TANIS, probably, as in line 4, 11.

10 THREE TIMES ; three strokes, with M,N, for 𝚺ΕΝ𝐓, *a measure.*

11 IN ; RO, the preposition, as in lines 2, 12, and 4, 9.

12   A DAY; R,E; ΡΗ, *the sun*.   The sun is often used as the D.S. of *day*, which supports this reading.

13   UPON; H,R,I; ϩΑΡΟ, but also spelt ϩΑΡΙ.   See line 7, 29.

14   IT; translated WHICH in lines 2, 11, and 3, 14, and 8, 39.

15   . SACRED ORNAMENTS.   Some of these may be ostrich feathers, as here represented.   Compare line 3, 11.

16   Some word of similar meaning; I,T ,E, with S,N, plural.   The Eye is a vowel, the letter I, in Antoninus, Appendix 72.   It is only in the word Osiris that it is an R, being there used instead of the mouth, the usual R.

17   This seems to be a plural noun followed by NEB, *all*.   The letters T,B, may be ORNAMENTS, allied to ΤΕϮΤωϦ, *to orna-ment*.   While the Greek is contented with a general term, we seem to have in the hieroglyphics a variety of words, more accurately describing the several ornaments.

18   RELIGIOUS CEREMONIES,, as in line 6, 7.

19   FOR; N, the preposition, as in line 3, 24, &c.

20   The OFFERINGS, represented pictorially by a table and a priestess sitting before it, with S,N, plural.   The arms held up represent a worshipper.

21   AS or LIKE; H,A,I; ϩΕ, *like*.

22   UNTO; N, the preposition.

23   The GODS, as in line 5, 8, &c.   The three strokes for the plural are here on the wrong side of the noun.

24   Of the COUNTRY, represented by characters for fields.   See line 8, 16.

25   IN; M, the preposition, as in line 4, 22, &c.

26   The ASSEMBLIES, as in lines 8, 19, and 10, 24, and 11, 12, and 12, 20.   The character represents a boat, with a canopy over it.

27   THE; P,E; ΠΙ, the article.

28   Probably HOLY DAYS, as we have the character for *god* joined to that often used for *day*.   See lower down.

29   UPON; H,R; ϩΑΡΟ, as in line 7, 13, but without the final vowel.

30   The DAY; E, for ΕϨΟΟΥ, followed by the sun, as at No. 12.

31   OR; N, the preposition ΝΑ

32   FESTIVAL, as in lines 10, 38, and 13, 33.   The first character here is not very distinct from that in line 8, 30.   But the two words are well distinguished by the hand, which here is open and holds nothing.   See Canopus 19, 15, and 18, 37.

33   AND; II,A; ⲁ2ⲁ, as in line 5, 28, &c.

34   IN; A,E; ⲉⲟⲩ, as in line 5, 3.

35   The DAY, as in lines 7, 30.

36   OF; M, the preposition, as in line 7, 25.

37   HIS NAME; ⲡⲁⲛϥ, as in line 6, 26.   As the king is always styled Beloved by Pthah, probably the day sacred to the god Pthah was his name-day.

38   IN ADDITION TO; M,O,T,O,T; as in lines 6, 8 and 9.

39   The CEREMONIES, of some kind or other.   Compare line 7, 20.

40   To PREPARE, or MAKE; more literally TO REGULATE.   This word is also *Steersman*, written over the man who steers the boat of the god Ra.   Voc. 1746.   Compare line 3, 3.

41   UNTO; N, the preposition, as in line 7, 31, &c.

42 and 43   KING; as in line 6, 14 and 15.

44   PTOLEMY, as in line 6, 16.

Line 8.

1   A PORTABLE STATUE, represented by a sitting figure, followed by the letter S, as in line 8, 25 and 32.   The final S may make the word into a diminutive, as STATUETTE.

2   A doubtful word, descriptive of the statue.   The second character is the staff, with a dog's head.   It is often held in the hand, in statues of priests and gods, as seen in the names of the Ptolemies, Appendix 50, 52.   Our characters may mean WITH AN ANUBIS-STAFF.   The M may be the preposition.

3   OF; M; ⲉⲗⲗ, the sign of the genitive case, as in Canopus 4, 13, &c.

4   GOLD.   The character represents a dish, with a cloth over it, in which the gold dust was separated from the broken stone.   See line 4, 1.

5   EVERY; Il; compare 2ⲏ, *the first*, and 2ⲁⲉ, *the last*.   See line 12, 18.

F

6 OF; M, the preposition.

7 EVERY TEMPLE; see line 14, 7, for the word *Temple*, a Sceptre followed by T, the article, and E, *a house*. The dish is ⲚⲓⲂⲓ, *every*.

8 OF; N,?,M; ⲚⲈⲖⲖ, the preposition.

9 EGYPTIANS; as in line 7, 1, where, however, the first syllable is wanting; and as in line 12, 32, where we have not the final letter of this group. Its literal meaning is not certain; but it is an Eastern figurative name for the people. It may be read ⲡⲱⲟⲩ, *mouths*, perhaps meaning ⲡ̇ⲡⲱⲟⲩ, *Kings*; E, perhaps ⲉⲟⲟⲩ, *glory;* the D.S. of *city* or *land*, and ⲚⲓⲂⲓ, *every;* followed by Ⲛⲓ ⲡⲁⲚ ⳁ, *his name;* or " kings of every glorious land is their name." On the other hand, the dish may be ⲚⲏⲂ, *lord;* and Ⲛⲓ ⲡⲁⲚ, when the final F is away, as in line 12, 32, may be meant for Ⲛⲓ ⲡⲱⲖⲖ, *mankind*, and then the whole becomes " kings of the glorious land, lords of mankind." In either case it is a boastful poetic name, and may be compared with Daniel viii. 9, and xi. 41, where Judea is, in the same figurative way, spoken of under the name of the land of beauty or glory.

10 The name of a place, or building, for which the Greek does not help us; O,M,B, with D.S. of a house.

11 To BE HONOURED; SEB,R; perhaps ⲱⲓⲂⲉ, *difference, excellence*, and ⲓⲡⲓ, *to make*. The first character is ⲤⲎⲂⲓ, *a sword*. See line 13, 43.

12 TOGETHER WITH; H,R; ⳅⲁⲡⲟ, as in line 6, 2.

13 The SHRINES, represented pictorially. The character differs from *Temple*, in line 3, 2, by having a bar across it, perhaps the means of carrying it. We have in the British Museum several of these small shrines, or models of a temple; about eighteen inches high.

14 OF; N,E; Ⲛⲁ, the preposition, as in line 5, 34.

15 The GODS; as in lines 5, 8, and 6, 3.

16 Of the COUNTRY, as in line 7, 24.

17 To be DONE; A,R,A,R,F; from ⲓⲡⲓ, *to do*, in a reduplicate form, followed by ⳁ, the pronoun of the third person singular.

18 On the DAY; as in line 7, 12, but unlike 12, 17, where the order of the characters is changed.

19   Of the ASSEMBLIES, as in lines 7, 26, and 11, 27.

20   GREAT; ⲭⲱⲡⲓ, in the plural, the adjective following its substantive. See line 5, 19, &c.

21   At the GOING OUT, represented pictorially by a serpent coming out of its hole. This ceremony is usually called "The carrying out."

22   Of the GOD, as in line 8, 15, &c.

23   FROM; M, the preposition, as in lines 11, 9, and 12, 31. This preposition is used for Of, From, and In.

24   The TEMPLE; literally a LIBATION-HOUSE; a vase pouring out water, followed by T, the article, and E, ⲎⲒ, a house. The final character, whatever its meaning, is in lines 8, 7, and 14, 7, the adjective which makes the House into a Temple.

25   The PORTABLE STATUE, as in line 8, 1.

26   OF; R, the preposition, as in line 7, 11, &c.

27   AMUN-RA; M,N,R,A; the first two letters are of an unusual form. Compare line 2, 19. Other inscriptions give to them an intermediate form.

28   HIS WATER-PROCESSIONS; a boat with S,N, plural, and with the pronoun, Ⳋ, preceding its substantive, instead of following.

29   IN ADDITION; as in line 6, 8 and 9.

30   SHALL CARRY OUT; ⲘⲀⳜ, to carry, preceded by S, for the future tense. The second character may be ⲘⲎⳜ, an anvil. The S is often used as the prefix of the future in the Decree of Canopus. The second character in this word is not clearly to be distinguished from that in Festival, lines 7, 32, and 10, 38. Here, however, the arm holds a stick, as in the word Receive, line 10, 40. See Canopus 33, 28, where is the word Carry, where the arm does not hold a stick.   .

31   The SHRINE; represented pictorially, as in 8, 13.

32   The PORTABLE STATUE, represented pictorially, and followed by the letter S, as in line 8, 25.

33   OF; N, the preposition, as in line 6, 6, &c.

34   GOD; as in line 8, 22, &c.

35   EPIPHANES; as in line 6, 22, &c.

36   LORD OF BLESSINGS; as in line 6, 23, &c.

37　ALL ; T,R, with S,N, plural ; **ⲦⲎⲢ**, *all*, the adjective following its substantive. See line 2, 7.

38　BY ; R, the preposition, as in line 5, 17, &c.

39　WHICH ; as in line 5, 6.

40　May be SHOWN ; see lines 13, 39, and 6, 24.

41　UPON ; O,T ; **ⲞⲨⲦⲈ**.

42　The SHRINE ; as line 8, 31.

43　THAT SAME ; T,N ; from **ⲦⲈⲚⲦⲰⲚ**, *to imitate*. The adjective following its substantive. See Canopus 24, 6.

Line 9.

1　The CROWN, that of Upper and Lower Egypt, being formed of the two crowns united, as in line 9, 17. In line 10, 10 and 11, we see them separate.

2　EVERY ; NEB ; **ⲚⲒⲂⲒ**, *all*. The Greek has "Ten crowns."

3　THE ; P,E ; **ⲠⲒ**, the article.

4　HEAD, being a head in profile, followed by E ; **ⲀⲠⲈ**, *a head*.

5　Of the SHRINE ; as in line 8, 31. The Shrine, or model of a temple, is to have a statue in it ; and on the head of that statue the crown is to be placed.

6　THE SAME ; as in line 8, 43.

7　IN ; M, the preposition, as in line 6, 8, &c.

8　MANNER, as in line 5, 4.

9　UNTO ; N, the preposition, as in line 8, 33.

10　The GREAT, in the feminine dual, made so by the T, T, each the feminine article. See line 5, 19. The adjective here stands before its substantive. It has a double termination, because that substantive is in the dual.

11　TWO ASPS, represented pictorially. The asp often represents a Goddess, and is a feminine noun.

12　APPOINTED ; as in line 10, 14, &c.

13　THE ; P,E ; **ⲠⲒ**, the article, as in line 9, 3, &c.

14　HEAD ; as in line 9, 4.

15　Of the SHRINES ; as in line 9, 5.

16　A ; A,O ; **ⲞⲨ**, the indefinite article.

17　CROWN ; as in line 9, 1.

18　M ; the preposition, as in line 2, 6, &c.

19 Perhaps IT; P,N, as in line 14, 2. In Canopus 2, 15, &c., these letters require this meaning. In the Rosetta Stone 11, 6, and 11, 29, this word is spelt A,P,N.

20 UPON; R,R,R; ⲉϩⲣⲁⲓ, as in line 2, 5. If we take that line as our guide, we should here read No. 20 and 18 as a compound preposition before the noun No. 19. But the uncertainty of the next word makes this conjecture doubtful.

21 Possibly BECAUSE OF, as in line 10, 12; ?,R; with the same meaning, it would seem, as R alone. It may be the preposition ϧⲁⲣⲟ.

22 WHICH; N,T,E; ⲛ̀ⲧ.

23 Possibly WHEN; P,S,T. A doubtful word.

24 ILLUSTRIOUS, represented figuratively by the sun and its rays. See line 10, 9.

25 HIS MAJESTY; so translated often in the Decree of Canopus. The bird is ⲟⲩⲣⲟ, *king;* the serpent, ϥ, *his*. Compare line 2, 1.

26 WENT BY BOAT; the boat followed by ϥ, the termination of the verb in the third person singular. See line 10, 5.

27 FROM or TO; M, the preposition.

28 The PALACE; represented pictorially.

29 MEMPHIS; P,T,H,M; Pthah, the god, and ⲙⲁ, *place*. Here perhaps we have the origin of the city's name; ⲙⲁ-ⲙ̀-PTHAH, *the place of Pthah.*

30 Perhaps HE ENTERED; S,I,N,F; ⲥⲓⲛⲓ, *to pass on,* with ϥ the termination *He*. See line 5, 11, for the first letter.

31 and 32. Doubtful words, possibly WEARING THE ROBES.

33 Possibly PRIESTLY; S,T,N, meaning belonging to the Soten, or priest.

34 The SOTEN, or chief priest; SO, with the D.S, of the priest wearing the crown peculiar to that order of priest.

35 OF; R, the preposition, as in line 8, 38, &c.

36 The TEMPLE; as in line 4, 10.

37 HE TOOK; CH,F; ϫⲓ, *to take*, with ϥ, the pronoun.

38 THE APPOINTMENT; T,SH; ⲧⲱϣ. This latter letter must not be mistaken for those in line 7, 24, and 8, 16. See line 10, 40, and also Canopus 8, 26. It is a weaver's frame, and

named from ⲱⲉ, *a beam*. See Canopus 3, 26, where it is better formed.

39   UNTO HIMSELF; N,F; ⲛ̀, the preposition, and ⲥ̨, the pronoun.

40   Of the KINGDOM; represented by a man wearing a crown, and the syllable ⲙⲉⲧ, which changes ⲟⲩⲣⲟ, *king*, into ⲙⲉⲧⲟⲩⲣⲟ, *kingdom*. See line 5, 18.

41   GREAT; C,H,R,T; ⲭⲱⲡⲓ, *great* in the feminine. The adjective to the foregoing substantive. The substantives beginning with ⲙⲉⲧ, are mostly, perhaps all, in the feminine.

42   IN; M, the preposition, as in line 6, 8.

43   ADDITION; as in line, 6, 9; O,T,O,T; ⲟⲩⲁⲅⲧⲟⲧ, *to add*.

44   WHICH; as in lines 5, 6, and 8, 39.

45   IN; M, the preposition or prefix of the case.

46   The PLACE; M,E; ⲙⲁ, *a place*, as in line 14, 27.

47   The PHYLACTERY, represented by a band round a head, and followed by the band itself.

48   OF; N, the preposition, as in line 7, 31, &c.

49   Perhaps SILVER, where the Greek has *gold*; P,A,T; ⲡⲓ ⲅⲁⲧ, *silver*, with the article.

50   WHICH; N,T,E; ⲛⲉⲧ, as in line 4, 12.

51   ON; M, the preposition, as in line 14, 22, &c.

52   Some parts of the crown or ornaments. But the Greek does not help us here.

53   Perhaps WHICH, as conjectured at line 7, 7. See also line 11, 29.

54   ON; M, the preposition as above. Or if the next letter, an A, belongs to it, it may be ⲙⲁ, *place*, as in line 9, 46.

55   Perhaps the SQUARE. The finger, ⲧⲏⲃ, being repeated three times, takes a final vowel as its plural termination, and thus may be used for ⲧⲉⲃⲓ, *a square*.

56   Of the CROWN, represented pictorially.

Line 10.

1   LOWER EGYPT, represented by the peculiar plant, as in line 5.

2   HE; P,E; ⲡⲓ, the pronoun and article. See line 7, 27.

3   Perhaps CELEBRATED, but the Greek does not help us. See

however, lines 11, 21, and 12, 22, which pretty well fix the meaning.

4   Perhaps a FESTIVAL, represented by an altar. See line 13, 17.

5   HE WENT BY BOAT, as in line 9, 26.

6   ALONE; P,O; ΠΟΥΑ, as in Canopus 12, 9, &c.

7   Perhaps SOLE LORD; MOU, NEB; ΜΑΥΑΑ, *alone*, and ΝΗΒ, *lord*.

8   Perhaps IMMORTAL LORD. See the words *Immortal Gods* in line 5, 8. This is the group translated by Hermapion *Lord of the diadems*, from the Obelisk. See Ammianus Marcellinus. The asp was the ornament of the royal diadem.

9   MADE ILLUSTRIOUS. The letters S,B,H, are of doubtful meaning. See *Illustrious*, line 9, 24.

10   UPPER REGION, distinguished by its crown, that of highest rank.

11   LOWER REGION, distinguished by its crown.

12   Probably BECAUSE OF. See line 9, 21. It may be the preposition ϨΑΠΟ; but the first letter is doubtful.

13   WHICH; as in line 9, 22, &c.

14   It is DECREED, as in line 1, 5, &c.

15   In the month of MESORE; being the fourth month of its season, and thus distinguished by four moons.

16   The LAST DAY; according to the Greek *the thirtieth* day; H, for ϨΑΕ, *last*, and the Sun, the D.S. of a day. See line 11, 8.

17   The DAY; E, for ΕϨΟΟΥ, *day*, followed by the D.S.; as in line 11, 5.

18   Of the BIRTH; M,S; ΜΑC.

19   Of the PRIEST, meaning the King; NOU,B; ΝΟΥΗΒ. See the letter B in the name of Queen Scemiophra, Appendix 10, and Labaris, Appendix 8.

20   LIVING, as in line 6, 17.

21   FOR EVER, as in line 6, 18. Here the last letter is well formed, and thus explains those places where we have a plain stroke instead of the wavy line.

22   KEPT, literally ESTABLISHED. See line 5, 20.

23   IN; M, the preposition, as in line 7, 38.

24   The Assembly, as in line 7, 26.

25   Perhaps Festival, as in lines 10, 38, and 7, 32.

26   Or; M, the preposition, as in line 9, 45.

27   Horus, represented by a Hawk, and distinguished by a whip, which is one of the sceptres of the god Osiris. He stands upon a perch, which is sometimes the letter T.

28   Probably Temples, but the characters are injured. Compare line 12, 30.

29   N,R ; ⲚⲈⲠⲈ, the prefix to a verb in the past tense. It may be read as Was done. See Canopus 15, 3.

30   In like manner, as in Canopus 15, 4; H, T, T, literally a copy, as in Canopus 34, 38; from ⲐⲈ, like. See line 13, 19.

31   Upon; R,R,R,N ; ⳜⲓⲠⲈⲚ, as in Canopus 15, 5. Compare also RRR, ⲈⳜⲣⲀⲓ, lines 2, 5, and 9, 20.

32   The month Paophi, represented figuratively as the second month of vegetation. Voc. 978.

33   The seventeenth day; the numerals Ten and Seven, preceded by T, the article, and the sun for Day.

34   He brought; I,N,F ; from ⲒⲚⲒ, to bring, with ϥ, the termination of the third person singular. See Canopus 26, 32, for the same verb, with a feminine ending.

35   The treasures; A,K,O ; ⲀⳜⲟ. The figure of a mummy may describe the treasures meant; but the Greek does not help us.

36   Belonging to; N,E ; ⲚⲀ, as in line 7, 4, &c.

37   The Chief priest; SO,T ; as in line 6, 14, and 9, 34.

38   On the Festival, as in line 13, 33, and 7, 32.

39   Or; M, the prefix of the case, or the preposition.

40   The Receiving; SH,P ; and the arm holding a short stick, which in line 2, 18, and Canopus 5, 40, &c., is figurative of receiving. See line 9, 38, for the force of the first letter. The whole is ⲰϨⲠ, to receive, as in Canopus 3, 26.

41   Or; as in line 9, 9, &c. ; or the prefix of the case.

42   The Kingdom; represented by a crowned man, and the word SO,T,A,A. This is a word derived from SOT, No. 37.

43   From ; M,A, or A,M ; ⲘⲀ.

44   FATHER; T,F,E. We do not find this word in Coptic.

45   HIS; F; ϥ, the pronoun adjective following its substantive, as in line 5, 26.

46   BEHOLD; A,A,S; or I,S, for the double A is often used for I; ⲓⲥ, *behold*. See line 13, 10.

47   Probably THE BEGINNING; R,F,P,E. From ⲁⲛⲉ, *the head*, with ⲣⲉϥ, the common prefix to make an adjective out of a substantive. The Greek has " the *author* of many blessings."

48   OF; M, the preposition, as in line 9. 18.

49   ALL THE OTHER; CH,T,O,NEB; ⲕⲉⲧ, *other*, and ⲛⲓⲃⲓ, *all*.

Line 11.

1   A doubtful word. But see line 4, 20, where these letters SH,T, are ϣⲟⲧ, *hard*.

2   A, the article; A,O; ⲟⲩ, as in line 12, 40, &c.

3   Perhaps PLACE; M,A,I; ⲙⲁ, *a place*. See lines 12, 42. and 14, 32.

4   CELEBRATED; I,O,T; as in Canopus 17, 21, and 19, 40, and 21, 16. The word is not found in Coptic. Perhaps it may be connected with No. 7, 16.

5   DAYS; as in line 7, 30.

6   WHICH, as in lines 11, 35, and 13, 34; A,P,N. In Canopus 2, 15, PN bears this meaning.

7   SEVENTEEN DAYS; the numerals as in line 10, 33, with the D.S. for DAY.

8   The LAST DAY, as in line 10, 16.

9   OF, the preposition, as in line 10, 26, &c.

10   EVERY MONTH. The moon and star, with T, form the word *month*; the ring is D.S. of time; and the dish is ⲛⲓⲃⲓ, *every*.

11   IN; M, the preposition, as in line 10, 48, &c.

12   The ASSEMBLY; as in line 10, 24, &c.

13   IN; M, the preposition, as in line 11, 11, &c.

14   The TEMPLES, as in lines 12, 30, and 14, 23.

15   OF; N,E; ⲛⲁ, the preposition, as in line 7, 4.

16   EGYPT; but why the tree hast hat meaning does not appear. It may represent a tree known to be of dark foliage; hence ⲭⲁⲙⲉ, *black*, for ⲭⲏⲙⲓ, *Egypt*.

G

17 Perhaps HEREAFTER, or at TIMES. This word is used five times in the Decree of Canopus, and there seems to bear this meaning.

18 IN ADDITION, as in lines 6, 9, and 8, 29.

19 Perhaps AND, as in line 5, 23; but perhaps part of the next word.

20 A doubtful word, but the last character resembles a libation.

21 Perhaps SHALL PERFORM; see lines 10, 3, and 12, 22, in which last place it has the same prefix. This begins with S,N,R; ⲚⲈⲠⲈ, the prefix of a past tense, and S, the prefix of a future tense. Together they seem to denote the future.

22 RITES; T,H, plural; ⲦⲀⲔⲞ, *things appointed*, as in line 12, 23.

23 AND; as in lines 4, 15, &c.

24 ALL OTHER; I,CH,T,NEB. Compare line 4, 6. Perhaps the Eye may be the final vowel in the foregoing word, ⲀⲔⲈ, and.

25 RELIGIOUS HONOURS; so translated often in the Decree of Canopus; T,O,T, from ⲦⲞⲨⲰⲦ, *an image.*,

26 TOGETHER WITH; N,I,M; ⲚⲈⲘ.

27 ASSEMBLIES, as in line 10, 24.

28 BY BOAT; M, the preposition, and the picture of a boat.

29 WHICH; as in line 11, 6.

30 MONTHLY, as in line 11, 10, but with the addition of the letters T,E, which in the case of ⲖⲀⲘⲠⲒ, *a year*, makes ⲈⲦⲈⲖⲀⲘⲠⲒ, *yearly.*

31 ALL OTHER; as in line 11, 24, but with the letter O in addition in this case. The O may be a plural termination.

32 CELEBRATIONS, as in line 11, 4.

33 IN; M, the preposition, as in line 10, 39.

34 ASSEMBLIES; as in line 10, 24.

35 WHICH; as in line 11, 29.

36 This letter S may perhaps be a part of the foregoing word. But more probably it stands for ⲒⲤ, *behold.* See lines 5, 2, and 10, 46.

37 The article, A,O; ⲞⲨ, as in line 9, 16.

38 ALL SCRIBES; S,E; ⲤⲀⲔ, *to write*, as in Canopus 15, 34 and 16, 3. It is followed by the word NEB, ⲚⲒⲂⲒ, *all.*

39   A doubtful word I,?T, with S,N, plural. Compare lines 7, 16, and 11, 4.

40   Perhaps the god Horus, represented by a hawk.

41   The TEMPLES, as in line 9, 86.

Line 12.

1—9   PTOLEMY, LIVING FOR EVER, BELOVED BY PTHAH, GOD EPIPHANES, LORD OF GOODNESS; as in line 6, 16—23, except that here the sculptor has carelessly omitted the M in the word **ЯΛEI**, *beloved*.

10   YEARLY, being the year of the seasons, distinguished from the civil year used in dates, and preceded by TE, as in line 13, 36. See Canopus 1, 1, and 7, 33.

11   The season of VEGETATION, represented by the standing plants. This season being of four months, if the natural season is meant, began about 15 Nov. But the first third of the civil year may possibly be meant.

12   FROM; A,M; **ЄΛΛ**, the prefix of the genitive case.

13   FIRST, a character used in place of the single moon in the first month of each third of the year. Voc. 991, 994, 998.

14   VEGETATION, as above. This, with the last character, makes the name of the month THOTH, which at this time began on 11 Oct.

15   The DAY; R,E; **PH**, *the sun.*

16   DURING; O,T,R; **ЄTPЄ**, *as*, but the first letter is doubtful.

17   FIVE DAYS; E,R, *day*, as in line 10, 17, followed by the numerals.

18   Perhaps EVERY REGION; **H**, *each*, as in lines 8, 5, and 14, 28. The second character may be thus explained by the help of the Greek.

19   A doubtful word; R,E, with S,N, plural; possibly the participle MADE, from **IPI**, *to make;* or possibly BEGINNINGS, from **PO**, *a mouth* or *opening.*

20   ASSEMBLY, as in line 11, 27, but preceded by S, for which the reason does not appear.

21   ALTARS; S,H,O,E; ϢΗΟΥⲈ, followed by the D.S. and sign of the plural. See line 4, 31.

22   SHALL CELEBRATE, as in line 11, 21.

23   RITES, as in line 11, 22.

24   AND, as in line 11, 23.

25   ALL OTHER, as in line 11, 31.   Compare line 11, 24.

26   RELIGIOUS CEREMONIES, as in line 11, 25 ; but here spelt with fewer letters.

27   WHICH; as in line 10, 13; but spelt with an additional vowel; N,I,T,E; ⲚⲈⲦ.

28   The PRIESTS, represented pictorially as men making libations, probably OTHPH, *dedicated*, from ⲞⲨⲞⲦⲈⲂ, *to make a libation*. See line 5, 33, and Canopus 1, 24.

29   OF; N,E; ⲚⲀ, *belonging to*, as in line 10, 36.

30   THE TEMPLES, as in line 11, 14.

31   OF; M, the preposition, as in line 11, 11.

32   EGYPTIANS, as in line 8, 9.

33   WEAR CROWNS, represented pictorially.   See line 4, 17, where this is part of the word *gold*, and line 5, 18, where it is part of the word *kingdom*, and Canopus 37, 18, where it is *conspicuous*.

34   PROCLAMATIONS.. Compare lines 8, 40, and 6, 24, and 14, 19.

35   The PRIEST; NOU,B; ⲚⲞⲨⲎⲂ.   This is the title of highest rank, and the king is the person here meant.   See line 8, 34, where we have the word *god* written by means of the hatchet ; and see line 4, 17 for this form of B.

36   EPIPHANES, as in lines 8, 35, and 6, 22.

37   LORD OF GOODNESS, as in lines 8, 36, and 6, 23.

38   M, the preposition, which with the following makes a compound preposition.

39   INTO or AT; E,R,O; ⲈⲆⲠⲞⲒ, a form of ⲈⲆⲠⲀⲒ.

40   The article, as in line 9, 16.

41   FORMULARIES; literally PRIEST—HOOD—THINGS.   See *priest* line 12, 28; and *priesthood*, in line 13, 1 ; and the sign of abstraction in *kingdom*, line 9, 40.

42   Compare line 11, 3, for this doubtful word.

Line 13.

1 The PRIESTHOOD; as in line 12, 41.

2 OF; N, the preposition, as in line 9, 9.

3 GOD; as in line 12, 6.

4 EPIPHANES; as in line 12, 7.

5 LORD OF GOODNESS; as in line 12, 8.

6 THE; as in line 10, 2.

7 SIGNET RING; CH,T,M; in Hebrew חתם, *a seal*, followed by the D.S. In Coptic we have ϩΙΤΕϨC, *to sign*. See Canopus, 12, 37.

8 The figure of some kind of priest, as in line 7, 39.

9 HANDS; T,T,E, with S,N, plural; ΤΟΤ, *a hand*.

10 BEHOLD; A,S; ΙC, as in line 5, 2.

11 IT IS MADE; A,R,E,F; from ΙΡΙ, *to make*, with ϥ, the sign of the third person singular.

12 Possibly GREATLY, meaning VERY; S,O; ϢΩ. See Voc. 656.

13 LAWFUL; COΥΤΕΝ, with a final S of uncertain value. Perhaps the sign of the future tense, as in line 13, 28; if so, IT SHALL BE LAWFUL. See line 1, 5.

14 To PRAISE; M,A,A,O,E; from ΔΙΔΙ, *to praise*, with M, the prefix of the infinitive mood.

15 APPOINTED PERSONS; as in line 13, 13, with the persons represented pictorially.

16 WHO; N,T,E, with S,N, plural N̄Τ. See line 9, 50.

17 Probably SHALL ATTEND TO THE ALTAR, represented pictorially, with S, the sign of the future tense.

18 To SET UP; as in line 14, 4.

19 A COPY; H,T,T; from ϩΕ, *like*, as in line 2, 4, and Canopus, 34, 38. See also line 10, 30.

20 SHRINE, represented pictorially, as in line 8, 42.

21 THAT SAME; T,N, from ΤΕΝΤΩΝ, *to imitate*, as in line 8, 43.

22 OF; N, the preposition, as in line 13, 2.

23 GOD, as in line 13, 3.

24 EPIPHANES, as in line 13, 4.

25 LORD OF GOODNESS, as in line 13, 5.

26 BY; the preposition, as in line 9, 35.

27 WHICH; as in lines 9, 44, and 7, 14.

28 IT SHALL BE LAWFUL; as in line 13, 13; with S, the sign of the future tense. The double N has the same force as the single letter.

29 IN; M, the preposition, as in line 11, 33.

30 TEMPLES, literally HOUSES; E, with S,N, plural, ΗΙ, *a house.*

31 ADDITIONAL; see in line 11, 18, &c. Here however, instead of O,T,O,T, we have M,O,O, with S,N, plural; perhaps from ΜΟΥΟΥΙ, *additional.*

32 Perhaps ALL; I, NEB, plural. It may be ΝΙΒΙ, *all,* though usually written with only the one character, as in line 4, 6, &c. Compare line 11, 24.

33 FESTIVALS, as in line 10, 38, and Canopus 18, 37, &c.

34 WHICH; as in line 11, 29, &c.

35 MONTHLY, as in line 11, 30.

36 YEARLY, as in line 12, 10.

37, 38 BY WHICH, as in line 8, 38 and 39, and line 13, 26 and 27.

39 IT IS SEEN, as in line 8, 40.

40 Perhaps WHY; O,T; the preposition ΟΥΤΕ, as in line 8, 41.

41 IT IS LAWFUL; as in line 13, 28, &c.

42 EGYPTIANS; CH,M,O, plural; ΧΗΜΙ, Egypt; TO, ΘΟ, *the land,* followed by E, ΕΟΟΥ, *glory;* T, the article, and the D.S. of a country or city; literally, " the Egyptians of the land of the glorious city." See Canopus 8, 31 and 32.

43 THEY HONOUR, literally, HE HONOURS; P,E; ΠΙ, *he;* and *honours,* as in line 8, 11. In Canopus 4, 37, this singular pronoun is used for the plural.

Line 14.

1 DECREES, literally WRITINGS; S,SH,O,E; CϪΑΙ, *letters.* See line 14, 16. The figure is a man in the act of showing, as in line

13, 39. The second letter, when better drawn, is the leaf of a water-lotus, 𝕆O, *a plant*, and hence an SH.

2   Probably WHICH; P,N, as in line 9, 19; perhaps the same as APN, in line 13, 34, &c.

3   THEY, literally HE, as in line 13, 43.

4   Shall SET UP; as in line 13, 18, though with a change of letter.

5   A TABLET, represented pictorially.

6   WHICH; N̄TE. See line 13, 16.

7   TEMPLE; E for HI, *a house,* preceded by T, the feminine article, and a sceptre of uncertain value. See line 8, 7.

8   Perhaps CARVED; O, perhaps, OℽⲀℰ, sometimes meaning *to add, to work.*

9   IN; M, the preposition, as in line 13, 29.

10 LETTERS, represented by a writer's pallet, and a pen tied to it.

11 FOR; N, the preposition, as in line 5, 10.

12 PRIESTS; as in line 12, 35.

13 LETTERS, as above.

14 FOR; N, the preposition, as in line 13, 22.

15 BOOKS, represented by a sheet of papyrus, ⲀⲬI, followed by A,I,H. See Canopus 34, 40, and 37, 12.

16 LETTERS; S,SH,A,A,H; CⲆⲀI, *a letter.* See line 14, 1.

17 FOR; N, the preposition as above.

18 GREEK, according to the Greek; but the flower is the usual character for Lower Egypt, as in line 5, 36. At this time Lower Egypt was very much peopled by Greeks.

19 PROCLAMATIONS. Compare line 13, 39.

20 WHICH; as in line 13, 38.

21 THEY SHALL SET UP; literally HE SET UP, as in line 13, 18.

22 IN; M, the preposition, as in line 11, 13.

23 TEMPLES, as in line 12, 30.

24 OF; M, the preposition, as in line 14, 9.

25 EGYPTIANS, as in lines 12, 32, and 8, 9.

26 CONSPICUOUS; as in Canopus 37, 18.

27 PLACE; M,A; ⲙⲀ, as below, and Canopus 37, 19.

28   EACH FIRST ; see *each* in line 12, 18,

29   EACH SECOND.

30   EACH THIRD.

31   OF ; R, the preposition, as in line 13, 26.

32   The BASE, or PLACE ; M,A, as above, and at line 9, 46.

33   Of the STATUE ; as in line 6, 11 and 12.

34—end. UNTO KING PTOLEMY LIVING FOR EVER, BELOVED BY
PTHAH, GOD, EPIPHANES, LORD OF GOODNESS.

APPENDIX.

KING'S NAMES,

With the Hieroglyphics explained by the help of the Greek Writers.

1.

Ch. O.F.O, the Cheops of Herodotus, Suphis of Manetho, Saophis of Eratosthenes. The F is ϩϥⲱ, *a serpent.*

2.

N.V. Ch. F.O. Nefchofo. The first two letters form the name of the god Kneph, the Ram-god. The Ram is a V in Sevechus, No. 30; but a similar animal, perhaps a goat, is an S in Vespasian, No. 67.

3.

First name; Ra, S,O,B.

Second name; A.M.N.M,T,R; Amunmai Thori, or rather Chori, as the T has the guttural sound of Ch; "Beloved by Amun, Strong." The M is ⲙⲉⲓ, *beloved;* T.R, ⲭⲱⲣⲓ, *strong.* See Nitocris, No. 15, for this last word. This is the Ammenemes of Manetho's IXth Dynasty.

4.

First name; Ra, Ho, K.

Second name; O,S.R.T,S.N, Osirtesen, or Osirigesen, if we give to the T a guttural force, as above; Geson Goses, of Manetho's Dynasty XII. The third letter is ⲣⲟ, *a mouth;* the last, N, is from ⲛⲟⲩⲛ, *the deep sea,* representing waves. The first letter, the Anubis-staff, like the figure of Anubis, is probably a vowel.

5.

First name ; Ra, Noub, Ko ; Noubkora, as the Ra is pronounced last, though placed first for pictorial reasons. The pair of arms is K ; but here we add the plural termination, because there are three of them. The dish is ⲛⲟⲩⲃ, gold; and this name is Chnubus Gneurus of Eratosthenes, which he translates *Gold the son of Gold.*

Second name ; as No. 3, Ammenemes II. of Manetho.

6.

First name ; Ra, Mes, Ho ; Meshora. The second character is ⲙⲉⲏ, *an anvil.* The beetle is Ho, or To; see Antoninus, No. 73.

Second name ; Osirtesen, as No. 4.

7.

First name ; Ra, Mes, Ko ; Meskora ; in Eratosthenes Moscheres, which he translates Heliodotus, agreeing with our first two characters, which, in the name of Rameses, Hermapion translates " When the Sun has tried."

Second name ; Osirtesen, as before.

8.

Ra, L,A,O,B ; Laobra ; Labaris of Manetho. The whole lion has the same force as the half of the animal in No. 3; and the R and the L are not distinguished in Coptic and Hieroglyphics. The last character is a B in Scemiophra, No. 10, and is the word ⲟⲩⲁⲃ, *holy ;* but why is not evident.

9.

First name ; Ra, N,S,M,A,T. For the S, see No. 10.
Second name ; as in No. 3. Ammenemes III. of Manetho.

10.

Ra, S,M,A,B,O, Smabora ; in Manetho Queen Scemiophra. The sickle is S, from ⲟϩⲥ, *to reap.*

11.

First name; Ra, K,P, Chebra. The second character should have a handle to be a K. In this form it is more usually NEB. The last letter is **ΑΠΗ**, *a head*, and hence P.

Second name; I,M,S, Ames; Amosis in Manetho, the first king of his Dynasty XVIII. The first letter is **ΙΟϨ**, *the moon*. This king is in Manetho followed by Chebros, whose name we recognize in this king's first name.

12.

First name; Ra, Shogsheg, K, Shogshegkara; in Manetho, Echescosokara. The second letter is from **ϬΟΧϬΕΧ**, *to kill*.

Second name; A,M,N,O, Th, Ph; Amunothph; in Manetho, Amenophthis.

13.

Second name; Thoth, M,S, Thothmes;—Mes, H, Ra; in Manetho, Mesaphris. For the Anvil, Mes, see No. 6 and 7.

14.

Second name; Thoth, M,S,—Mes, Ho, B; in Manetho, Misphragmuthosis, in which word we recognize the Mesaphra of the former name.

15.

First name; Ra, Mi, K, Mikera; the Mikerinus of Herodotus, a king who built the third pyramid, but here a queen, the wife of No. 14. The sitting figure, with the ostrich feather on her head, is **ΜΗΙ**, *truth*.

Second name; A,M,N,N,T,T,R, Amun Neith Thori or Gori; in Eratosthenes, Nitocris, which he translates Minerva the victorious, our Neith-gori.

16.

Ra, Men, Ko, or Ra, M, Ko; Menkora, or Mikora. This is the name found in the third and fourth pyramids, and is that of the king who built them. It is nearly the same as the first name of Queen Nitocris, No. 15, and also as the first name of her step-son, No. 17.

17.

First name; Ra, Men, Ho; Menhora, or, if we place the definite article before the word Ra, as is usual, Menhophra. Menhora closely agrees with Menkora, No. 16; and Menhophra is the king who gave his name to the era, B.C. 1322, when the Sothic period began.

Second name; Thothmes, Hob.

18.

Second name; Amunothph, as No. 12; meaning *Devoted to Amun*. Eratosthenes translates it Ammonodotus. The last syllable is ⲱⲧⲃ̄, *to pour out a libation*.

19.

First name differs from No. 17, only by adding the three dots, the vowel O, to the beetle, which of itself is Ho.

Second name; Thothmes Mesmeso, or *victorious in battles*, from ⲙⲁϣⲩ, *to wound*.

20.

M,T,M,S; Mautmes, or *tried by the mother goddess*. The ship is ⲭⲟⲓ, perhaps S, as it is sometimes interchanged with other forms of the S.

21.

Second name; Amuno, the short of Amunothph, No. 18, and followed by a title, perhaps "Lord of some city." This king is the maker of the musical colossus; and his name is written both Amenophis and Amenothis by the Greeks.

22.

First name. Here the sword, which in No. 12 we read as ⲥⲟⲭⲥⲉⲭ, we must read as ⲥⲏⲃⲉ, *a sword.* The sun, ⲡⲏ, with the article, is Phra. And we recognize this name in Semphracrates, or Seb-phra-krot, of Eratosthenes, which he translates as Hercules Harpocrates. Whether the beetle represents Horus, or ⲫⲣⲟⳁ, to complete the name, or whether the last syllable is to be found in the second name, is doubtful. The latter half of this name means "Approved," but its sound is unknown. See No. 53.

Second name; Amunmai, followed by Hor, N,M, Neb. This may be the Horus of Manetho.

23.

Second name; Ra, M,S,S,O; Rameses of Manetho.

24.

First name; Ra, Men, Mi.

Second name; Pthah, M, Osiris, I,N. This king, the father of Rameses II., is Osymundyas in Diodorus, and hence we may read it as Osi,men,thah. He is also Amenophath in Manetho; hence, if the figure of Osiris is an O, it becomes Oimenpthah. In some cases we have the dog-headed god, Anubis, in place of Osiris; the name then is Aimenpthah. Eratosthenes reads it Chomaephtha, thus using a guttural; and he translates it as "The world beloved by Pthah," mistaking Cho for ⲑⲟ, *the world.*

25.

First name is translated by Hermapion, "Whom the sun approved." The first three characters are Ra, A, Mi, and may be Amun Ra, the god. The latter characters are translated as "Approved" in No. 53, the name of Ptolemy Epiphanes.

Second name; Ra, Amun, M, M,S,S, Amunmai Rameses, translated by Hermapion "Whom Amun loves, and the sun has tried."

We omit the later Theban kings of the family of Rameses, and turn to those kings of Lower Egypt whose names have been quoted by the Greek and Hebrew writers.

26.

Second name; Amumai Shishank, the Shishank of the Bible. His name in Hieroglyphics is spelt with and without the N. The Sh is from ϩⲟⲉ, *a plant.*

27.

Second name; Amunmai O,S,R,K,N; in Manetho, Osorthon. The difference may have arisen from the doubtful force of the guttural. The K, the dish, in our cut should have a handle to it.

28.

Second name; Amunmai, T,S,S,E; T,K,L,E,M,T. Of these letters the first four mean Son of Isis. The throne S, with a T over it, is Isite; the Egg and stroke are SHE, for ϣⲏⲣⲓ, *son.* The remaining letters form Takelmot; in Manetho, Takellothis. The last letter is ⲧⲉⲃ, *a finger,* and hence a T.

29.

Second name; S,B,K,O,T,P; Sabacothph, or "Devoted to the God Sabak." See the word ⲱⲧⲃ̄, in No. 18. Manetho calls this king Sabakon.

30.

First name; Ra, B,K; probably Bocchoris; as this Ethiopian conqueror may have adopted the name of the native king whom his predecessor dethroned. See No. 10 for the B.

Second name; S,V,K, Sevechus in Manetho.

31.

Second name; T,E,R,K; in Manetho, Tarachus; in
the Bible, Tirhakah. The Lion was an L in No. 8; the
two letters were not distinguished in Egypt.

32.

First name; Ra, B,B; perhaps Bophra, or Vaphra, a
name that Manetho gives to one of his successors.

Second name; P,S,M,T,K, Psametick; in Manetho,
Psammetichus.

33.

First name; Ra, B,B, nearly the same as in No. 32.
The leg, ϕⲀⲦ, may be B,V, or F.

Second name; N,K,O; in Manetho and the Bible,
Necho.

34.

First name; Ra, II,B; in the Bible, Hophra; in
Manetho, Vaphra.

Second name, as in No. 32.

35.

First name; Ra, N,B, perhaps Nephra, as we meet with
a successor of the name of Nepherites in Manetho.

Second name; A,M,N,T,S; Amasis in Manetho, to
which we must add, Son of Neith. The Goose, like the
Egg in No. 28, is the word *Son*.

36.

K,N,B,O, Sh; Cambyses. The N and M are often interchanged.

37.

Second name; N,T?,R,I,O,S; Darius. The vase is N; the legs, on which it stands, T. The two represent D, as in No. 70; and as MP represent B. The second character may be A.

38.

First name; Ra, Neb, To; *the sun, the lord of the world.*

Second name; M,N,T,O,O,T,P; Mando-othph, or *dedicated to Mando,* the god of Mendes. This king is not mentioned by the Greek historians.

39.

Ch, S,I,R,S; Xerxes.

40.

Second name; A,T,N, Ra, B, Ch, N; *the servant of the lord Ra;* ⲂⲰⲔ, *servant;* ⲚⲀ, *of;* ATEN, perhaps from the Hebrew אדן, *lord;* and ⲢⲎ, *the sun.* This may be the name called Inarus by Thucydides.

41.

First name; Pharaoh, written with as many as seven letters; then H,A,O,M,R,A, probably Thannyras, who, on the death of Inarus, was, according to Herodotus, the governor of Egypt for the Persians.

Second name, of three words, each following an M; RNF, ⲢⲀⲚϤ, *his name;* M,O, Ch, N,T,I, perhaps ⲘⲞⲨϢⲒ, *successor,* ⲚⲦⲈ, *of;* Atenra, the late king.

There is a difficulty about fixing the date of these two names; but the number of the letters, and their ornamental character, show that they are thus modern.

42.

N,F,A,O,R,O,T ; perhaps Nepherites of Manetho.

43.

Second name; A,M,A,A?,T,K, possibly Amyrtæus, 'who reigned'at the same time as Inarus..

44.

Second name; E,K,A,R,I ; Achoris, in Manetho.

45.

First name; Ra, O,S, possibly Osiris. If so, the whole is " Approved by Osiris and Pthah."

Second name; P,S,M,T; Psammuthis in Manetho. The child places his hand to his mouth to mark that he is an infant, and does not speak.

46.

First name; Ra, Ho, K ; perhaps Achoris, borrowed from No. 44.

Second name; N,O, Ch, T,A, Neb, FO; Nectanebus in Manetho.

47.

First name ; Beloved by Amun, approved by Ra.

Second name ; P,L,I,P,O,S; Philip the brother of Alexander the Great.

48.

First name; Beloved by Amun, approved by Ra.

Second name ; A,L,K,S,A,N,T,R,S. Alexandros, the son of Alexander the Great.

I

49.

P,T,O,L,M,Æ,A,S; Ptolemæus.

50.

First name of Ptolemy Philadelphus; Beloved by Amun, to whom Ra gave victory. This translation is learned from No. 53.

Second name, as No. 49.

51.

First name of Ptolemy Euergetes; Son of the Brother gods, approved by Amun, a living image of Ra. This translation also is learned from No. 53. The thigh, ϭⲡⲁ, *a bone*, from joint to joint, with the meat on it, may stand for ϣⲏⲣⲓ, *son*.

Second name; Ptolemy living for ever, beloved by Pthah. ·

52.

First name of Ptolemy Philopator; Son of the gods Euergetæ, approved by Pthah, to whom Amon gave victory, a living image of Ra.

Second name; Ptolemy, living for ever, beloved by Isis.

53.

First name of Ptolemy Epiphanes; Beloved by the two gods, approved by Pthah, to whom Ra gave victory, a living image of Amun. See line 3 of the Greek of the Rosetta Stone for this translation.

Second name; Ptolemy, living for ever, beloved by Pthah, as in line 4 of the Greek of the Rosetta Stone.

54.

First name of Ptolemy Philometor; Son of the gods Epiphanes, approved by Pthah and Horus, an image of Ra and Amun. The Beetle is Ho, followed by the mouth ρω, to make Horus. The last two letters are I,M, ⲓⲚⲓ, *an image;* the M for N.

55.

First name of Ptolemy Euergetes II.; Son of the gods Epiphanes, approved by Pthah, an image of Amun, a living image of Ra.

Second name; Ptolemy, beloved by Pthah, living for ever. The standing figure is the god Pthah.

56.

Two versions of the first name of Ptolemy Soter II. The cross in the first is the word Soter. It is followed by T,S, the termination of a feminine name. We perhaps should there read, " Son of the Queen Soter," as if his mother, who reigned jointly with him, also bore the name of Soter.

57.

The name of Cleopatra and her son Ptolemy Alexander.

First; K,L,A,O,P,A,T,R,A, followed by T,S, the feminine ending of many names.

Second; P,T,O,L,M,A,A,S; then T,H,N, which may be conjectured to be ⲦⲀϨⲈⲙ, *surnamed;* A,L,K,S,N,T,R,S; living for ever, beloved by Pthah.

58.

Berenice and Ptolemy Alexander.

First ; a title followed by B,A,A,R,N,I,K, with T,S, the feminine termination.

Second ; P,T,O,L,M,A,A,S ; then T,O,H,T,T,N, which must be understood to mean Surnamed, and seems to contain the words ⲧⲟ, *given*; ⲉⲓⲧⲟⲧ, *in addition*; ⲛ̄, *of*; A,L,K,S,N,T,R,S, living for ever, beloved by Pthah. See Canopus, line 12, 17, for the word ⲉⲓⲧⲟⲧ. But see No. 57, where the letters between the two names are not the same.

59.

The name of Ptolemy Neus Dionysus.

60.

K,L,A,O,P,A,T,R,A, with T,S, the feminine termination ; H,T,N,S, probably *immortal*, being ⲉ,ⲏⲧⲉⲛ, *the end*, with S, a feminine termination ; T,R,P,I,N,O; Tryphæna; and the figure of Amun.

61.

Cleopatra,   and   her   son   Cæsarion ; K,L,O,P,T,R,A,S, and K,I,S,R,O,S ; both names being in the Greek genitive form.

62.

First name of Augustus Cæsar; A,O,T,O,K,R,T,R; Αυτοκρατωρ.

Second name; K,I,S,R,A,S; living for ever, beloved by Pthah and Isis.

63.

First name of Tiberius Cæsar; T,A,B,A,R,A,A,S.

Second name; K,A,S,A,R,S; ⲚⲦⲈ, *who*, or *the*; Ruler. This last word is also Steersman of a boat; see Voc.

64.

First name of Caligula; King of Kings; A,O,T,O,K,R,T,R, Autocrator; beloved by Pthah and Isis.

Second name; K,A,I,S, Caius; K,I,S,R,A,S, Caisaros; K,R,M,N,I,K,S, Germanicus, living for ever.

65.

First name of Claudius; King of Kings, Autocrator.

Second name; T,B,R,S, Tiberius; K,L,O,T,I,S, Claudius.

66.

First name of Nero; Approved by four kings, beloved by Ra, and Amun.

Second name; Autocrator, N,A,R,A,N,I.

67.

A,I,S,P,S,A,N,A,S, Vespasianus, followed by a crocodile, meaning perhaps Egyptian, and the word Ruler. See No. 30, where the Ram is a V; but here the animal may be a goat, ⲟⲧⲉ, and hence an S.

68.

A,O,T,K,R,T,R, Autocrator; T,I,T,S, Titus; K,S,R,S, Cæsaros.

69.

First name; A,O,T,O,K,R,T,R, Autocrator; K,I,S,R,S, Cæsaros.

Second name; T,O,M,T,I,N,S, Domitianus; N,T, ⲛ̀ⲧⲉ, *who*, and Osiris's sceptre, probably meaning *Pius*, a not uncommon title with the Roman emperors; K,R,M,N,I,K,S, Germanicus.

70.

First name; Autocrator; K,I,S,R, Cæsar; N,O,A,I, or perhaps, N,O,HOR,A, Nerva.

Second name; T,R,A,A,N,S, Trajanus; perhaps Pius; K,R,M,N,K,S, Germanicus; I,N,T,I,K,K,S, Dacicus. In these words, as is often the case, the letters are put out of order for artistic reasons; and the D is written NT, as in Darius, No. 37.

71.

First name; Autocrator Cæsaros Trajanus, as above. Second name; A,T,R,A,N,A,S, Hadrianus; the Ruler.

72.

First name; Autocrator Cæsaros, as above.

Second name; A,N,T,N,I,N,I,S, Antoninus; S,B,S,T,S; Σεβαστοs.

73.

First name; Autocrator Cæsaros, as above.

Second name; A,N,To,N,I,N,S, Antoninus; H,R,O,I,A,S, Aurelius, the Ruler. In No. 6, No. 17, No. 54, &c., we gave to the Beetle the force of Ho; it sometimes is ӨO, as in the title Lord of the world. In Aurelius the H and R are united into one character.

74.

First name; A,O,T,K,R,T,R, Autocrator. The dish, to be a K, ought to have a handle. The R is as in Autocrator, No. 72; but here in a more ornamental form.

Second name; K,A,M,T,S, Commodus, living for ever. The K is the same as in No. 30, No. 33, and many earlier names; but here we have the whole man, not simply his arms.

75.

K,N,T,A,K,A,A, with T,S, the feminine termination; Candace, the Ethiopian queen. Here the sculptor has very carefully given us the basket, usually NEB, in place of the second K. The two characters are easily mistaken one for the other.

www.ingramcontent.com/pod-product-compliance
Lightning Source LLC
Chambersburg PA
CBHW020226090426
42735CB00010B/1598